A gift to Lyndsey Reimer
from Grandma + Grandpa Reimer
April 1990.

A gift to Lyndsey Reimer
from Grandma + Grandpa Reimer
April 1990.

MY PONY BOOK

Overleaf right A young rider practises leading her Shetland pony in-hand.

Overleaf left The wise and kindly head of a Haflinger pony, flaxen mane blowing in the breeze, wearing a traditional headcollar decorated with brass fittings.

MY PONY BOOK

SUE ALLFREY

WARD LOCK LIMITED · LONDON

© Ward Lock Limited 1984

First published in Great Britain in 1984
by Ward Lock Limited, 82 Gower Street,
London WC1E 6EQ, a Pentos Company.

All Rights Reserved. No part of this publication may be reproduced, stored in a retrieval system, or transmitted, in any form or by any means, electronic, mechanical, photocopying, recording, or otherwise, without the prior permission of the Copyright owners.

Designed by Andrew Shoolbred
House editor Suzanna Osman Jones
Text set in Photina
by Servis Filmsetting Limited Manchester

Printed and bound in Spain by
Graficromo, S.A., Cordoba

British Library Cataloguing in Publication Data
Allfrey, Sue
  My pony book.
  1. Ponies – Juvenile literature
  I. Title
  636.1'6   SF315

ISBN 0-7063-6304-3

Photographs by:
Sarah King: front jacket.
John Elliot: pages 66 below and 87; Kit Houghton: page 91 below; Peter Landon: pages 58-59, 67, 71 and 78; Leslie Lane: pages 42 below, 47 below, 50, 54, 55, 74-75, 91 above, and back endpaper; Sally Ann Thompson/Animal Photography: pages 6, 15, 19 below, 31 below, 34 and 82; Ron Willbie/Animal Photography: page 31 above; VNU, The Netherlands: frontispiece, pages 19 above and 30; Taylor Vrooman: pages 103 above right, 107 above and 110; permission of the Trustees of the Wallace Collection: pages 10-11. All other photographs by Sarah King.

Front endpaper: Ponies graze peacefully beneath a steely-grey Dartmoor sky.
Black endpaper: Four riders and a dog ford a river in the Highlands of Scotland.

Contents

1	**EVOLUTION AND HISTORY OF THE PONY**	6
	Origins, evolution, conformation in present day, change from utility to leisure role	
2	**PRINCIPLE BREEDS OF EUROPE**	17
	By country, history of development, original purpose, description of breed today	
3	**PRINCIPLE BREEDS OF AFRICA, AMERICA, ASIA AND AUSTRALIA**	34
	By country, history of development, original purpose, description of breed today	
4	**LEARNING TO RIDE**	41
	Clothes, riding on roads, balance, aids, seat, hands, exercises, paces, jumping	
5	**PONY CARE AND EQUIPMENT**	61
	Keeping a pony at grass, keeping a pony stabled, rugs, feeding, ailments, grooming, tack	
6	**ORGANIZATIONS AND RIDING FOR PLEASURE**	81
	The Pony Club, Horse Rangers, Endurance Horse and Pony Society, pony trekking, hunting	
7	**PONY COMPETITIONS AND EVENTS**	93
	Mounted games and gymkhanas, eventing, show jumping, dressage, showing, hunter trials	
8	**WORKING AND HARNESS PONIES**	109
	Horse-drawn vehicles, breeds of harness pony, the working pony today, Riding for the Disabled	
	ADDRESS LIST	119
	GLOSSARY	120
	INDEX	121

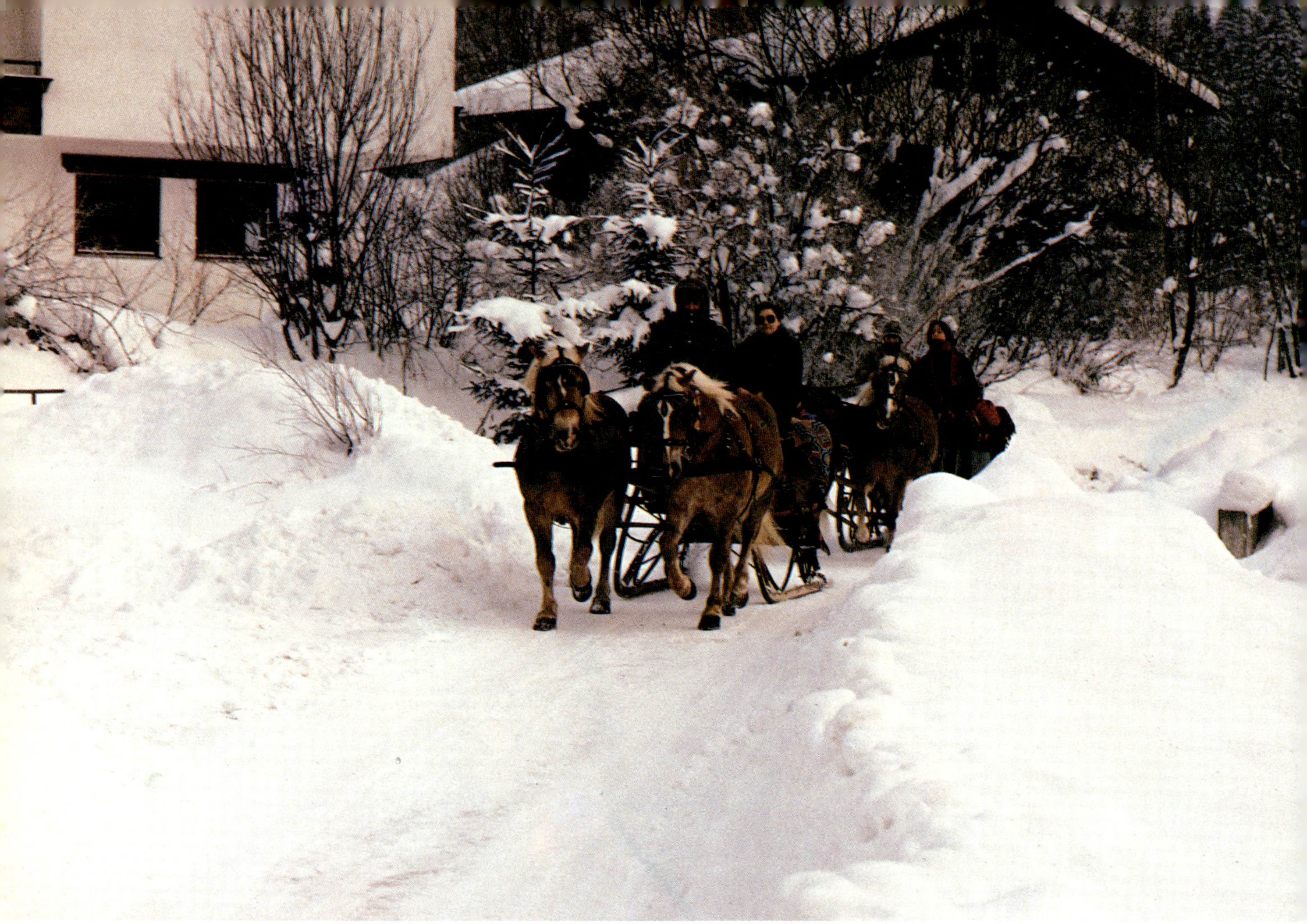

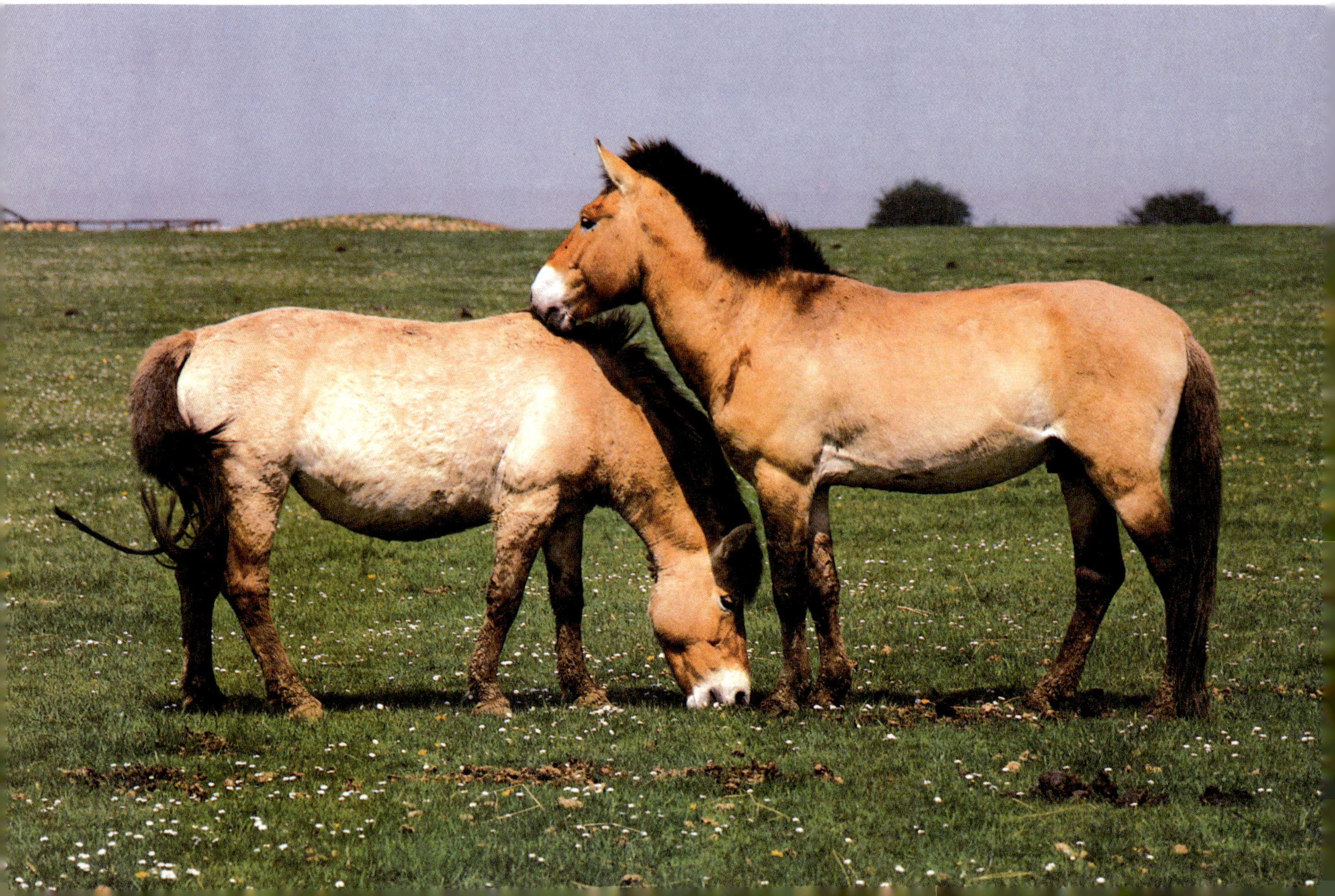

1
EVOLUTION AND HISTORY OF THE PONY

Left A long way from their original home in Mongolia, these Przewalski Horses are in Whipsnade Zoo, Bedfordshire. This breed is always a shade of dun, here a yellow dun.

Above left These sturdy Haflinger ponies are bred on the National Stud in Austria. The 'Fohlenhof' was originally the foal barn, and is now the guest house. In summer these ponies are used for light farm work and mountain treks; in winter, with the insides of their feet larded, and wearing special shoes, they draw sleighs across the snow.

EVOLUTION AND HISTORY OF THE PONY

Today's horses and ponies are descended from a completely different-looking animal that used to roam the world about sixty million years ago, before man had come down from the trees and started to walk upright. The four thousand years that man has been associated with the horse is in fact only a very small portion of time in the history of the horse itself.

These very early horses, known as *Eohippus*, were only about the size of a fox or a little larger, and had four toes on the front feet and three on the hind feet, each ending in a miniature hoof. At that time the sea was lower than it is now, and there were land bridges linking North America with Asia, also across the Mediterranean and linking Britain with Europe; *Eohippus* was able to roam throughout most of the world, with the exception of Australia and some islands.

As the millions of years passed these animals slowly changed, until they became somewhat like the horse of today. Their teeth developed from the stage of being suitable for browsing on leafy shrubs, until the horses were able to graze on the tough prairie grass. Their feet also changed a great deal; the fourth toe on the front feet disappeared and slowly the centre toe developed and enlarged to take most of the weight. Very many of the different lines of horse that developed became extinct, but some continued and adapted. By ten million years ago an important ancestor of the horse had developed, known as *Hipparion*, it was larger than *Eohippus* and travelled extensively throughout Europe, Asia and Africa as well as North America.

Gradually a one-toed animal known as *Pliohippus* developed in North America and from this descended the ancestor of today's horse *Equus Caballus*, which was probably about the size of a Shetland pony, and as shaggy, but slower moving. It depended on surviving by outwitting its pursuers and by being constantly alert. For the first two hundred thousand years *Equus Caballus* could spread from its home in North America into Asia, Europe and Africa; but during the next six hundred thousand years the Ice Age changed this. During that time vast areas as far south as present-day London and New York become covered with great sheets of ice and snow, killing the vegetation and driving animals thousands of miles further south. Many varieties of horses and other animals became extinct during the Ice Age. Horses also became aware of a new enemy, man, because they formed an important part of *man's* diet, and piles of horse skeletons have been found near some cave dwellings. The largest of these measured about 13.3hh, so by then horses had increased in size quite considerably.

When the earth became warmer and the ice melted, the sea-level rose, and about ten thousand years ago, the land bridges between America and Asia, across the Mediterranean, and between Europe and Britain, were submerged. Thus animals were no longer able to move from one continent to another as they had done. After this time horses appear to have survived best in Europe and Asia, in a wide belt north of the great mountain chains of the Alps and the Himalayas.

Following the Ice Age four main primitive types of horse emerged. One was the *Forest* horse in Northern Europe, a heavily built solid type with a big heavy head;

from these descended the 'cold-blooded' horses (the heavier breeds e.g. Shire and Percheron) of Europe. The second was the *Steppe* horse, lighter in build and more of a pony, standing about 12hh, which came from Asia and North Africa, and was the ancestor of the Oriental breeds (the Arab and the Barb). The third was the *Plateau* horse which originated in Siberia, Northern Asia and in Europe; this together with the *Steppe* horse are the ancestors of the warm-blooded breeds (Thoroughbreds and Hanoverians). The fourth type is the *Tundra*, which has practically no influence on present day breeds with the exception of the Yakut breeds in Russia which lives in the polar regions.

The two breeds that have best survived from these four primitive types are the Mongolian wild horse and Tarpan ponies which will be described later in this chapter, see pages 6 and 14.

First use of ponies by man

It is not known exactly when horses or ponies were first domesticated by man. It is probable that at first primitive people captured foals and brought them up in captivity; and then slowly began to realize the great potential that the horse offered. At first they probably only supplied meat and milk, then man discovered that they could be used for transport. It is known that horses were driven before they were ridden, and the earliest written records so far discovered report nomadic horsemen making raids 4,250 years ago. So we can assume that horses were first domesticated some while before then.

Horses were used for hunting by the Persians, Egyptians and Assyrians, several hundred years before Christ, at first driven in chariots and later ridden across country after gazelle and wild boar.

Use of ponies in wartime

In early times, any tribes who had tamed and learnt to ride horses had an enormous advantage over those tribes that had not. The mounted herdsmen of Mongolia, Manchuria and Eastern Siberia did ride horses, and armed with bows and arrows spread west and south, capturing land and towns as they went. The horse has played a very large part in the history of the world; those who were best mounted usually won the battle or war, so very great importance was attached to the horses owned by a country or a race of people, from those very early days until motorized transport took over from the horse less than a century ago.

The first war-horses were in fact only of stunted pony size and were used to convey warriors by chariot. Many centuries passed with kings and leaders trying to develop larger and stronger animals that would be suitable to carry warriors clad in armour on their backs. But it was not in fact until the Middle Ages that the magnificent chargers depicted in our history books appeared on the scene.

The mighty armies of Genghis Khan (1162–1227 AD), from Mongolia, were mounted on ponies, probably very similar in appearance to the Mongolian Wild Horse of today. The advantage that his soldiers had over their enemies by being mounted helped him to conquer the great dynasty over which he ruled, a huge area of Asia and Europe stretching from the Pacific Ocean to the River Danube.

Use of ponies in peacetime

Ponies were also used for sport and entertainment. Not only were they employed for hunting, but they were also used in chariot races. They were not really the magnificent horses seen in films such as *Ben Hur*; they were a much smaller and probably rather poor type of pony that certainly could not gallop as fast as today's horses do. However, it was by the crossing of the different breeds and types that bigger and better horses were developed.

'The Arab Tent', painted in 1865 by Sir Edwin Landseer (famous for the Trafalgar Square lions). It is considered a very faithful portrait of the Arab breed, particularly in the mare's kindly expression and large beautiful eyes.

Although ponies, and then later horses, played such an important part in the history of the world by taking part in wars, it has been as beasts of burden and transport that they have probably served man best. They were first used by the nomadic tribes as pack ponies to move their tents and cooking utensils from one grazing area to another. The Roman Empire depended on pack-trains for its commerce, and in England a regular pack-horse service was still running between Exeter and London in the 1690s. In some areas of the world today ponies are still used to transport goods to areas where no mechanized transport can go, such as in the mountains of Tibet and Mongolia, and parts of South America. So for over four thousand years, ponies have helped man to move goods from one place to another.

The pony of today

Horses and ponies have been used for so many different jobs throughout the world since they were first domesticated, that it is only possible to mention a few, in Chapter 8. What is remarkable is how ponies have changed and adapted from those first ancestors with several toes, to the many and varied breeds that can be found throughout the world today. It is worth therefore taking a look at the ponies of today to see what aspects of their make and shape are important.

'Conformation' means the make and shape of horses and ponies, and will differ considerably according to the functions they are expected to perform. A pony that has to carry a pack over mountainous terrain, or haul loads on a farm will not require the same conformation as one that is used as a show pony, or for dressage. However, all ponies should have some points of conformation in common. The outlook of the head and eye is important; a neat head with a large bright eye will usually denote a kind and intelligent pony. Avoid the pony that lays its ears back, bares its teeth and rolls its eyes, showing the whites when you approach. It has probably been ill-treated at some stage in its life, but it is also probable that it will never be safe to really trust under all circumstances.

A good straight and level backbone is also important; a pony that is lopsided to the left or the right will always have problems with balance. Also to be avoided is a pony with a *roach* back, one that stands a little like a greyhound with its back humped. Equally a pony is not a good prospect if it has a *sway* back, an excessive dip behind the withers; this is more frequently seen in horses that have been raced very young than in ponies.

A pony used for riding should have a good sloping shoulder and well-developed wither, with quite a long neck. A harness or pack pony will need a more upright shoulder so that he can throw his weight forward on to his forehand more easily. Hence some breeds used as pack ponies have developed with an upright shoulder and short neck, whilst those that are used for riding have been developed with the different requirements in mind.

All ponies should have a good depth of girth to allow plenty of *heart* room. This really means plenty of room for the lungs to be able to expand and develop so that the pony will have strength and stamina. The quarters should be well developed with plenty of depth from front to back and the tail should be well placed, not too low as seen in some poor specimens of ponies. Bone structure is always important, but never more so than of the legs; the cannon bones should be short and flat, the knees flat and the hocks and fetlock joints strong.

The feet are also of the utmost importance; the horn should be hard and the feet well formed and round. Avoid buying a pony with shallow feet or brittle horn. The age-old saying *No foot, no horse* is a very true one. A pony should also stand square on his legs, with the front legs not too close together, nor stand with the hindlegs too close or too far away from the front legs.

While conformation is important for ponies for both working and riding, it is even more important for breeding stock. Except where horses or ponies run completely wild, man has always endeavoured to use his best animals for stallions. Both stallions and mares, apart from having good conformation, should have a pleasant temperament, should move well and should be typical of the breed. It is of great importance not to breed from any stock that has any hereditary defects.

The Arab and its influence on horses and ponies

It would be incomplete to write any book concerned with breeds of horses or ponies without mentioning the Arab. The oldest of all the recognized breeds in the world, the Arab has had more influence on horses and ponies everywhere than any other breed. The most valuable of all horses, the Thoroughbred, has descended directly from the Arab. In fact it is true to say that all Thoroughbred stock throughout the world (approximately half-a-million), together with the millions of part-bred horses, have all descended from three Arabian stallions imported into Britain at the beginning of the eighteenth century. These Oriental horses were crossed with the now-extinct native Galloway pony (from N.W. Scotland); then selective breeding of the offspring eventually resulted in the Thoroughbred that we know today. The word Thoroughbred (a literal translation of the Arabic *Kehilan* meaning *pure bred all through*) was not used until 1821; and it was much later that the English Thoroughbred became established as a breed.

It is impossible to say when the Arab became established as a breed; Arabian people were pictured with horses earlier than 700 years BC; but it may well be that the Persians (in what is now Iran) were breeding these horses before that time.

Horses have played a close and important part in the life of Arabian people for centuries, helping to shape their way of life and their history. The stories of their great powers of endurance and their achievements in war have been handed down from one generation to another. Many leaders and rulers are remembered because of the fame of their horses.

Today the Arab horse is bred throughout the world; the danger facing his future is that his great popularity could result in careless over-breeding, with the production of inferior stock lacking the true Arabian characteristics. King Hussein of Jordan, anxious to preserve the true desert Arab, has undertaken a careful policy of breeding at the Royal Stud since 1961. He now has some truly magnificent stock with indisputable ancestry and beauty.

It has been found that Arabian horses have the ability to improve practically every other breed with which they are crossed. Their beauty and speed are probably better remembered than the other characteristics; but it is their great stamina, intelligence, hereditary soundness, and wonderful temperament with a great love for human companionship, that they transmit to other breeds.

India was probably one of the first countries where the Arabian influence was first noted. At the beginning of the thirteenth century Marco Polo tells of the shiploads of Arabian horses that were sold for great sums of money. Crossed with the native Indian ponies the offspring were found to have remarkable powers of endurance. The descendants of these ponies were used by the army officers as polo ponies, showing great speed and stamina.

The Arabians imported to Britain have also been of great consequence. Apart from founding the Thoroughbred, they have also been crossed with many of the native breeds of pony, improving the stock by passing on their stamina and soundness as well as their beauty and temperament. Several Arabian studs of great importance were established in Britain, most notably that at Crabbet Park where Wilfred Scawen Blunt and his wife Lady Anne Blunt imported stock direct from the tribes of the Arabian desert, during several trips, the first made in 1878. The Blunt's daughter Lady Wentworth continued the stud and imported a fine

Polish stallion in 1920, founding a new 'dynasty'. By 1909 there were ninety-six stallions standing at stud at Crabbet Park; this awakened a great interest in the breed, since when many magnificent studs have been developed throughout the world.

Whilst the greatest influence of the Arab has probably been on horses (because of the development of the Thoroughbred), there are few breeds of pony that have not had Arab blood introduced at some stage. Indeed, Arabs could almost be considered ponies, the stallions mostly standing 14.2–15hh, the mares a little smaller. They do, however, have the characteristics of a horse rather than of a pony, and are regarded as small horses.

Much has been written about the good and bad points of Arabian horses, but one indisputable fact is that they are regarded as the most magnificent of all horses or ponies, inspiring writers, painters and poets from time immemorial. A particularly striking painting shows an exquisite grey Arab mare and chestnut foal lying in an exotic eastern tent, with hunting dogs and monkeys looking on; it is by Landseer and hangs in the Wallace Collection, London.

The Arab head should be very short and refined, with the characteristic *dished* face, the muzzle exceptionally small and soft, the nostrils large and elastic, so that they can flare out with excitement. The eyes must be large and dark; they should be set wide apart and are lower in the head than in other horses. The jaw bone is very rounded, and set wide apart, so that a clenched fist will fit between the jaw bones. The ears, set well apart, are small, well defined and alert. The neck must have a distinctive arched curve, formed by the angle at which the head and the neck join. This feature is peculiar to the Arab, and determines the amount of movement of the head. The mane and tail hair, also a distinguishing feature, must be fine, silky and soft.

The neck should be long enough to give a good length of rein, the shoulder sloped and long, the chest broad, the back short and slightly concave. The loins are particularly strong, the croup wide and level and the tail set on high. The bone structure of the Arab differs from other horses, as they have fewer ribs and lumbar bones. A good Arab should have great length from hip to buttock and the gaskins should be strong and prominent.

The Arab has a greater density of bone than any other breed; the limbs are strong and clean with well-defined tendons. The knees are flat, the cannon bones short, the pasterns set at a good angle leading to near-perfect feet, any fault in this region being regarded seriously. Although the hindleg is not the strongest point of the breed, good Arabs are straight in the hindleg, the hocks set low to the ground and following the line of the leg.

The *floating* action of the Arab is one of the most distinctive characteristics of the breed. They must have great freedom of movement at all paces, and appear as though they are moving on springs. The trot, with little or no knee action must be full, free and generous, without the exaggerated 'daisy-cutting' action that predominates in the show-ring.

The Arab can be considered the prince among horses, and it is by retaining the purity of the breed that they can be used to improve other breeds in the future.

There are two more breeds that should be included in this chapter of evolution; they bear little resemblance to the Arab, but are the two remaining breeds of the primitive types of horse still in existence.

The Mongolian Wild Horse or Przewalski Horse

The last survivor of the Plateau horse was only discovered in 1881 by Colonel N.M. Przewalski, who found a small herd on the edge of the Gobi desert. They are the

This magnificent high-spirited Arab was bred in Russia. Many fine Arabs are produced there by a careful and selective breeding programme.

last truly wild horse that no one has attempted to domesticate. Although they are called horse, they are in fact what we know as a pony, standing only between 12 and 14hh. See page 5.

Unfortunately, since they were discovered they have been hunted, and as a result their numbers have been greatly diminished. Hunting is now forbidden by law, and there are quite a number in zoos throughout the world, Whipsnade in Britain, and Prague, for example. They have great powers of endurance and have existed on very sparse vegetation in the steppe and mountainous regions of Mongolia, where the climatic conditions are very severe. They are powerfully built with a large, quite short but heavy head. The ears are long, the mane short and upright with no forelock. The neck and back are short, the shoulders straight, and there is very little indication of a wither. The quarters are poor but the legs short and strong with large shallow feet with good horn.

Always a shade of dun with a black mane and tail and a black dorsal eel-stripe, they have mealy colouring round the muzzle and eyes, as do the Exmoor ponies. The ponies from Mongolia, China and Tibet have descended from these wild ponies, and therefore many of the breeds in Indonesia can trace their history to Przewalski's horse.

The Tarpan

The last survivor of the primitive Steppe horse, the Tarpan, lived on the Southern Russian steppes, in Eastern Europe. There were two types, the Steppe Tarpan which was found in herds south of the Ural Mountains, and the Forest Tarpan which once roamed the forests of central and eastern Europe. Some of the wild Tarpans were domesticated by the peasants, but their flesh was regarded as a delicacy and they hunted the wild ponies almost to extinction in the nineteenth century.

In Poland the authorities have set up two special reserves, in Bialowiecz Forest and at Popielno, where the Tarpan ponies are once again allowed to live wild. There is also a herd at the Science Centre where their remarkable resistance to disease is being studied.

Standing about 13hh, the Tarpan pony has a long broad head with a bulge around the nostrils. They have longish ears, a short thick neck and a good shoulder. The back tends to be long with a high wither, the quarters are poor and sloping with a low set tail. The legs are long, fine and hard. The colour usually varies between brown-dun and mouse-dun, with a black dorsal eel stripe, black mane and tail and zebra markings on the legs. In winter some Tarpans grow a long, almost white coat.

2
PRINCIPLE BREEDS OF EUROPE

PRINCIPLE BREEDS OF EUROPE

Whilst nearly all the European countries have their own breeds of horses, there are some countries who have no native breeds of ponies of their own at all. Britain must be the envy of pony breeders throughout the world, with more native breeds than any other country. At the other end of the scale, Belgium, Denmark and Holland have no native breeds and have had to import from abroad; whilst France, Germany, Italy, Spain and Portugal have very few native breeds still in existence. There are ponies in the Greek Islands, but these are rather poor specimens and have little consequence other than as local beasts of burden.

Right 'White horses of the sea', the Camarguais, cantering along the sands of their marshy homeland.

Below right The Exmoor makes a hardy, surefooted childrens' pony. This pair, bred on a stud, show the characteristic 'toad eye', mealy muzzles, underbellies and insides of thighs.

AUSTRIA

The Haflinger

One of the oldest breeds, the Haflinger is a native of the Austrian Tyrol, the name being taken from the village of Hafling, the centre of an area which is now part of Northern Italy.

These sturdy mountain ponies trace their ancestry back to both Arabian and cold-blooded breeds, which make them equally suited to light draught work as well as to being ridden. They are extensively bred throughout Austria, the young stock being raised on the Alpine pastures, which helps them to be hardy whilst developing their hearts and lungs and proving the soundness of their feet and legs. The stallions are all owned by the state; the colt foals undergo a rigorous inspection, and only about twenty will be chosen to remain as stallions each year. Haflingers are now bred in many other countries, Germany, Switzerland and Holland being the most important.

Standing between 13 and 14.2hh, the Haflinger has a distinctive colouring, always palomino or a shade of chestnut, usually with a flaxen mane and tail. They are thick-set with plenty of bone and are exceptionally strong for their size. They are capable of carrying great loads in mountainous country and are used regularly on many farms in high altitudes throughout Europe. They are equally amenable to bringing hay down from the alpine pastures, hauling firewood and being ridden. They make excellent driving ponies, transporting tourists in both summer sunshine and winter snow. See page 7.

Their attractive colouring makes them popular as riding ponies, whilst their sturdy conformation and quiet disposition has proved them most suitable as mounts for disabled riders.

FRANCE

The Camargue

The 'white' horses of the Camargue live in the swampland of the Rhône delta, from whence they take their name. These ponies live wild, existing on a diet of tough grass and salt water; occasionally they are rounded up for branding, when some will be kept to train as cow ponies, for farm work, or for holiday-makers to ride.

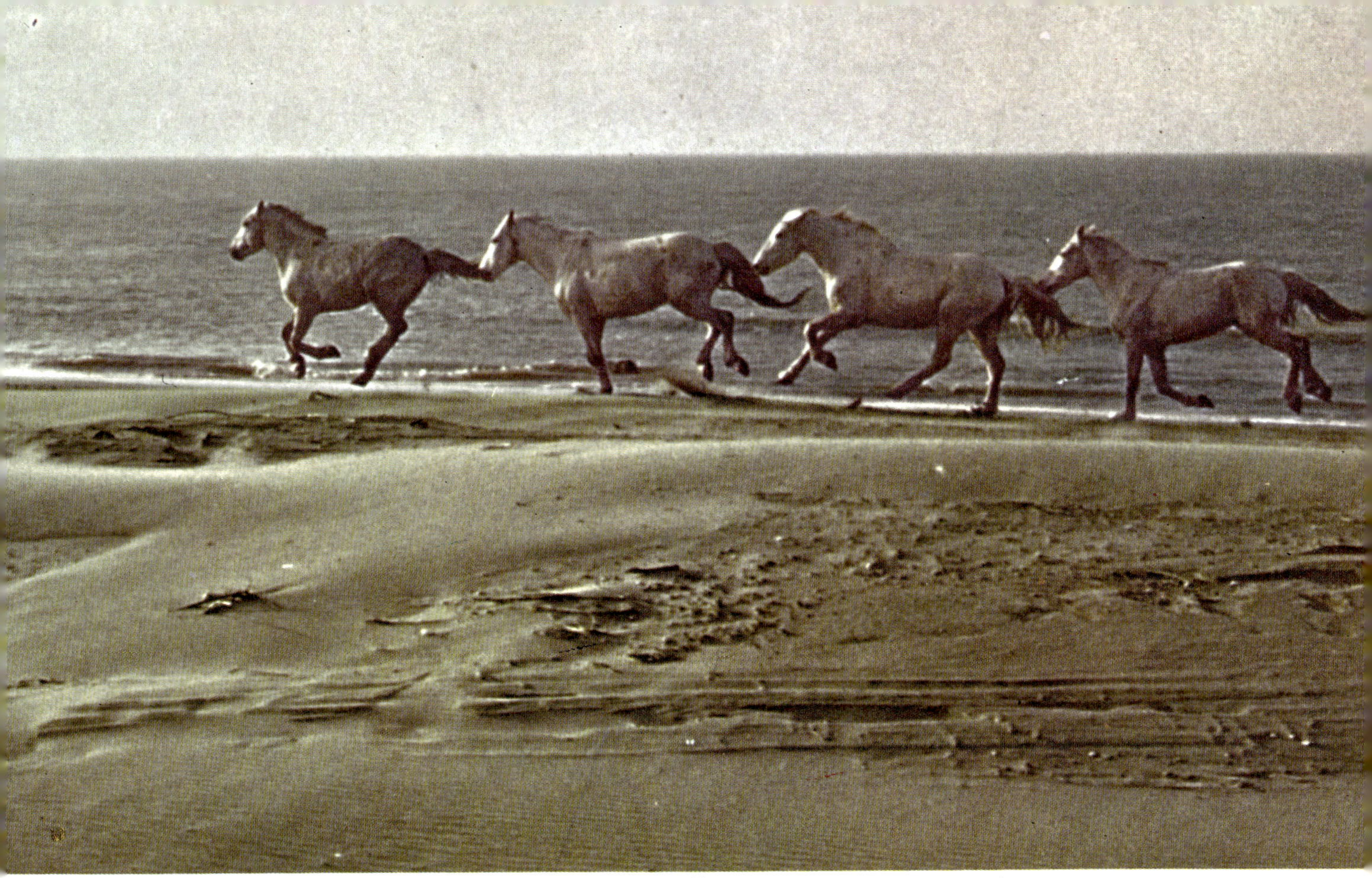

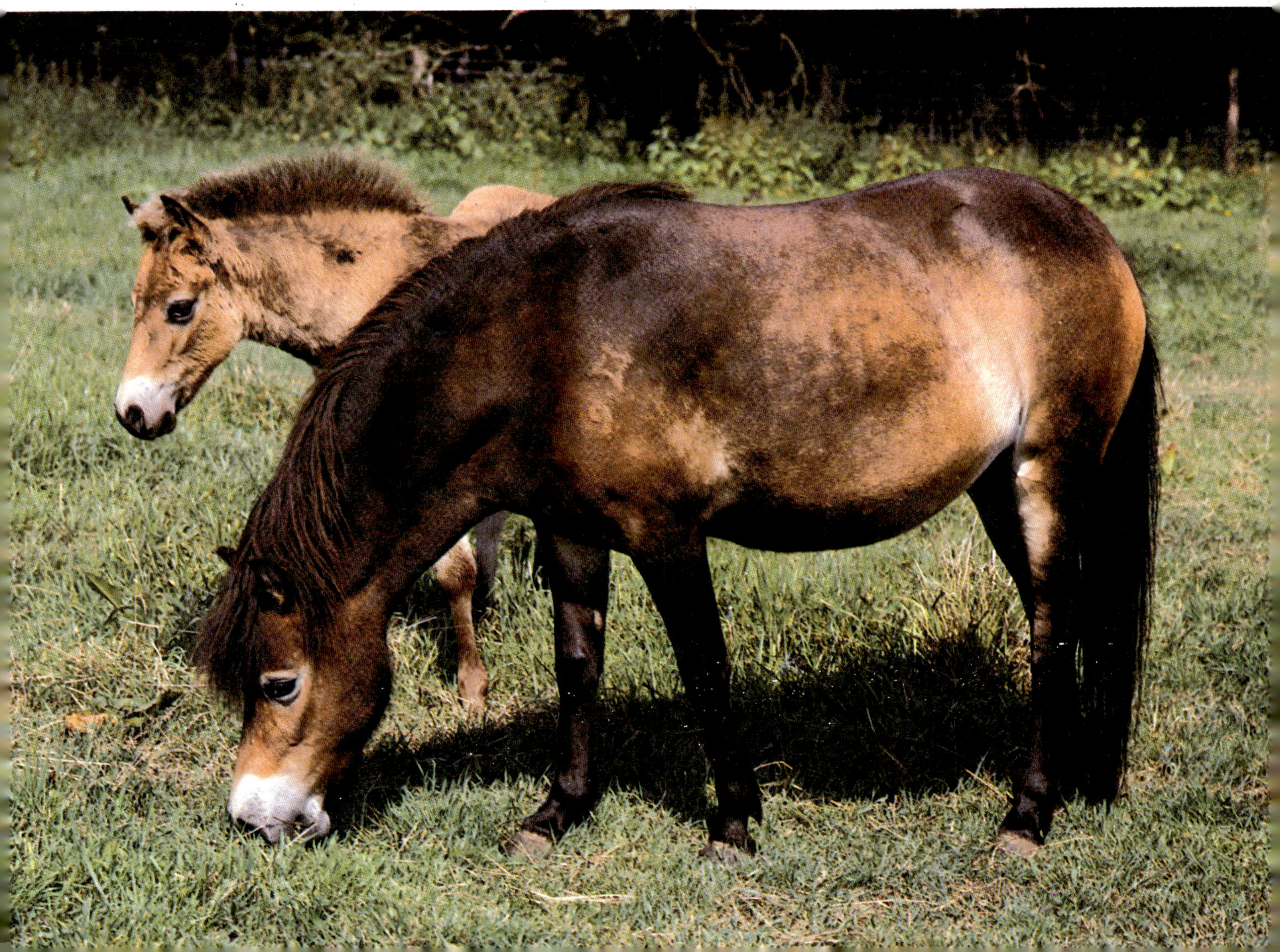

The uneven, sparse terrain, bleak in winter and hot and dry in summer, has produced a tough surefooted breed with an instinct for survival.

The foals are born dark (like the famous Spanish Riding School Lipizzaner horses), but lighten with age until they develop the characteristic white coat, which has made them known as the *white horses of the sea*. *The White Stallion* is a film about a Camargue horse.

Standing 13.2–15hh, these tough ponies have rather poor conformation, with a rough coat, large square head and upright shoulder. They are, however, noted for their short back, depth of girth and strong limbs. They have a characteristic high-stepping walk and a great ability to twist and turn, which makes them excellent mounts for the *gardians*, the local cowboys who herd the famous black bulls.

GERMANY

The Dülmen

The only remaining native pony of Germany, the Dülmen is still popular and is bred in the Meerfelder Bruch region of Westphalia, near the Dutch border, on the estate of the Duke of Cröy. These ponies run in a semi-wild state, first being mentioned in 1316, but, as pony stallions from Poland and Britain have been introduced, the breed is not really pure. Standing 12–13hh, these ponies tend to have a short neck and back and rather upright shoulder. They can be any colour although bay, brown and dun are the most common. There are about a hundred mares at present; they are rounded up annually and yearling colts caught and sold.

GREAT BRITAIN

The Shetland

The most northerly of the British native breeds, the Shetland is also the smallest. Originating in the Shetland Islands, situated about 100 miles (160km) north of the mainland of Scotland, these ponies have been exported to almost every part of the world. Exposed to the fiercest of the Atlantic weather, the vegetation of these islands is very sparse, with no trees, and the only shelter is to be found in the small valleys or behind rocks. As a result the ponies have to be very tough to survive, only the fittest withstanding the harsh winter conditions.

For hundreds of years Shetland ponies have played a vital part in the life of the crofters, acted as packponies for carrying the peat, and provided the only form of transport, both ridden and driven, until comparatively recently.

During the middle of the nineteenth century there was a great demand for pit ponies to work in the mines. Shetlands proved ideal, being small enough but also strong, and economical feeders. The heavier type of pony was therefore bred especially for the mines; however, with the introduction of mechanization, the demand for them ceased and there was a great decline in their numbers.

Standing only 8.2–10.2hh, the Shetland is the strongest of all the native breeds for its size. The most usual colour on the islands is black or dark brown, but numerous other colours have been bred throughout the world. A good Shetland should have a refined head, sloping shoulder and short strong back. Their legs are very hard with short cannon bones and tough, well-shaped feet. They have developed a very dense coat and profuse mane and tail to protect them from bleak winter weather.

The Highland

A native of the North of Scotland and the Western Isles, the Highland pony is a very old breed who has been associated with the crofters for centuries. There are two basic types of Highland pony. The larger, heavier type is found mostly on the mainland, and stands up to 14.2hh; it has, in the past, had infusions of Clydesdale blood. There are also smaller lighter types found on many of the islands in the Hebrides; these are not individual breeds, but do have characteristics from the different islands. Several islands have introduced Arab blood in the past, and these ponies tend to be smaller and lighter in build.

These highly intelligent sturdy ponies have for centuries played an indispensable role in the life of the crofters, being used as general utility ponies in the craggy islands. They are very surefooted and capable of carrying great weights over the roughest terrain. They are still used to cart stags during the deer-stalking season, but more recently have been in demand for pony trekking.

Standing between 13–14.2hh, the Highland is a sturdy compact pony. The head must be shapely, the large eyes set wide apart, the muzzle soft and velvety with wide set nostrils. The ears are small, the neck well arched, the legs short and strong with plenty of bone. The mane and tail hair should be soft with a little silky hair on the fetlocks. The most usual colours are one of the many shades of dun, grey or black. Most of them have a dark dorsal eel-stripe down their back, some also having zebra markings on the legs.

The Dales

The heaviest of the British breeds, the Dales ponies come from the east side of the Pennine range in Northumberland, County Durham and Yorkshire. They are very like the Fell ponies, having come from the same original stock. There is also the influence of the Welsh Cob, all Dales tracing back to a Welsh Cob stallion who was introduced about 100 years ago.

They were used for all forms of farm work and shepherding and make excellent harness ponies, being good trotters and capable of pulling great weights. The introduction of cars and tractors saw a great decline in the breed, hundreds being slaughtered for meat. Over the past twenty-five years, however, there has been a revival in the breed as their use for pony trekking has been appreciated.

Dales must not stand more than 14.2hh; they should have a compact body, neat pony head, short back, deep girth and well developed quarters. Great importance is attached to sound limbs and clean hard feet. The Dales is black, dark brown or occasionally grey in colour, with profuse mane and tail and silky feather on its heels. There should be no white markings other than a small star or snip on the forehead.

The Fell

Very like the Dales ponies in many ways, the Fell ponies, as their name implies, come from the fell area, the Lake District in Cumbria. They were extensively used by the local farmers, for pulling the family trap, shepherding on the hills and general farm work. During the seventeenth and eighteenth centuries they were used extensively as packponies, carrying loads of up to two hundred-weight (100kg) of lead from the inland mines to the ports on the north-east coast of England. They were also used for the local sport of trotting, when the work for the week was done. With the introduction of mechanical transport, the breed became in danger of extinction; but with enthusiasm from breeders they have been kept alive, and are now extensively used for pony trekking and make excellent driving ponies.

Fell ponies stand between 13 and 14hh. They are very strong and have exceptional stamina. The pony-like head is carried high, the well-sloped shoulder giving a good ride. A good depth of girth, compact body with plenty of bone combined with sensible temperament, hardiness and surefootedness make it an

excellent mount in its own countryside. Colours are black, dark brown, dark bay or occasionally grey; there is very little feather and very few white markings are allowed.

These delightful light chestnut Shetland foals have to be hardy to survive on the sparse vegetation on their native homeland.

Welsh breeds

There are four distinct types (known as Sections A, B, C, and D) of Welsh ponies which all come under different sections in the Welsh Stud Book. Recognized as some of the most beautiful ponies in the world, they all originate from the Welsh Mountain Pony (Section A). Ponies have bred on the hills in Wales for centuries, from original Celtic stock. They are extremely hardy and surefooted. Some infusion of Arab blood is said to be responsible for the slightly *dished* face and fiery elegance that these ponies have inherited.

The Welsh Mountain Pony (Section A)   Probably the most popular, as well as the most attractive children's riding pony in the world, the Welsh Mountain Pony has roamed the hills since the Roman times. Although through the centuries outside blood has been used in Wales, this, the smallest of the four types, has been the least influenced. The combination of intelligence, courage, gentleness and endurance, linked with an ability to jump, make them excellent children's riding ponies. They frequently excel in the show ring as leading-rein ponies, and are equally at home being driven in harness.

A Welsh Mountain Pony must not exceed 12hh. The characteristics are an exquisite head with small neat ears and large wide set eyes, set on a graceful neck. The short back couples the deep sloping shoulder with good quarters and well set-on tail. The clean legs are short and very strong, with dense flat bone and small hard feet. Grey is now the most common colour, but any colour other than piebald or skewbald is acceptable, as with the other sections of the breed.

Welsh Mountain Ponies are now bred throughout Britain, being the most popular of all the native pony breeds. They have been exported all over the world,

Above This Highland pony, showing an abundant mane and tail, is a fine example of this ancient breed.

Left A Dales pony stallion showing the good bone of this sturdy breed.

Below A prize-winning Fell pony in superb condition, thoroughly groomed for the occasion.

and several other countries now have their own Welsh Mountain Stud Books. They are one of the most popular pony breeds in Australia, for instance.

The Welsh Pony (Section B)   The Welsh Pony has been bred specifically as a child's riding pony. They inherit many of the characteristics of the Welsh Mountain Ponies but are larger, standing up to 13.2hh. They have been developed from the Welsh Mountain Pony and the Welsh Cob with crosses of Thoroughbred. They were used for shepherding on the hills, but today the heavier cob types are favoured for this job, and so they have been developed as riding ponies. The characteristics are similar to the Section A, but there is not so much knee action, and the movement comes from the good sloping shoulder.

There are probably few children's show ponies today that do not have some Welsh blood in their veins; most riding ponies have been developed by crossing these ponies with small Thoroughbred stallions. It is the only native pony, other than the New Forest pony, that may be shown plaited and trimmed in breed classes at shows – the other native breeds must have their manes and tails left untrimmed and just brushed out.

The Welsh Pony of Cob Type (Section C)   These ponies have also descended from the Welsh Mountain Pony and have Andalusian blood which was introduced in the twelfth century from Spain. When the Stud Book was first published in 1902, two sections were given to Welsh Cobs, the distinction between the two being one of size. Section C, the smaller of the two, must not exceed 13.2hh the same height limit as for Section B.

Welsh Ponies of Cob Type are the least numerous of the four Welsh sections. The main breeding areas are in Breconshire and Radnorshire. These ponies have most of the same characteristics as the Welsh Mountain Ponies, but are a larger, heavier version. They have a small neat intelligent head, good shoulder, short back with good depth of girth and powerful quarters. They are a much heavier and stockier pony than the Section B's, with more knee action.

They are used as they have been for hundreds of years, by shepherds on the mountains. They also make excellent trekking ponies and children's hunters, proving very tough, surefooted and sound. Their good free trotting action also makes them ideal driving ponies, a sport for which they are becoming increasingly popular.

The Welsh Cob (Section D)   The largest of the native breeds of pony in Britain, these eye-catching animals usually stand between 14.0 and 15.1hh. Again based on the Welsh Mountain Pony, these ponies have Andalusian blood and were a well-established type by the early sixteenth century. They are mostly bred around Cardiganshire and Pembrokeshire, and probably have gained their size by being crossed with the Pembrokeshire packhorse.

They have great presence and good looks, accompanied by an equable nature, and the inherited stamina to live out and thrive on relatively little food. All Welsh Cobs should have natural *fire* and action, which comes from the powerful muscular body and hock movement. Once used as general farm horses, they are today being bred extensively for riding. They make excellent hunters and general riding horses, being natural jumpers and having great staying power.

They have equally earned themselves a reputation as great trotters, being used for this pastime in years gone by; races were held when the general farm work was finished. They are still much prized as harness ponies, proving themselves outstanding in the different aspects of present-day driving. They are used singly, in pairs and in teams. See pages 110 and 118.

The Exmoor

Concern has been shown recently that the oldest of the British native breeds may be in danger of extinction. Ponies have bred on Exmoor, in North Devon, since pre-historic times, but there are now only three main herds left on the moors. Exmoors are bred in studs in other areas, but they tend to grow larger and lose their type when not in their natural environment.

The height limit for mares is 12.2hh although the stallions may stand 12.3hh. These very strong sturdy ponies have had to be hardy to survive the harsh climate they experience on the moors. Their exceptional strength comes from the deep wide chest, powerful loins and excellent clean limbs. The good hard feet help the ponies' ability and surefootedness over difficult terrain. Although so small, they are quite capable of carrying a full-grown man for most of the day, being used by the farmers for shepherding and to follow hounds. They tend to be rather nervous, but, properly handled, make good riding ponies.

The Exmoor is a breed with very little colour variation, all ponies being bay, brown or mouse-dun, they all have a distinctive mealy muzzle, and mealy-coloured markings round the eyes. They have unique *toad* eyes, the heavy top lids giving a hooded look. No white markings are allowed, but the coat is paler on the belly and the inside of the thighs. The head is short and thick-set, with wide set ears and eyes, giving these ponies a kindly and sensible look. The coat is short, wiry and almost waterproof; the tail is also distinctive, being very thick with a fan-like growth at the top known as an *ice* tail.

The Dartmoor

The Dartmoor has evolved geographically as a very close neighbour of the Exmoor, coming from South Devon, but it has several different characteristics. Like the Exmoor it has to be hardy to cope with the great variations in climate; it is also surefooted, quickwitted and intelligent.

The Dartmoor pony must not exceed 12.2hh. Although strong, well-made and good-looking, it is not as heavy as the Exmoor. The small, alert head, with neat ears, is carried quite high on the well-developed neck and shoulder. These characteristics are probably developed from infusions of Arab and Welsh blood at the beginning of the century. The back and loins are strong, the limbs clean with excellent bone and the feet particularly well shaped. Black, bay and brown, with only a small amount of white, and occasionally a grey, are the acceptable colours.

When small pit-ponies were required the breed became endangered, because Shetland stallions were turned on to the moor to breed smaller ponies. This random cross-breeding did not seem very successful. However, private breeders maintained the pure breeding stock which is in much demand today. An ability to think for itself, together with its kind, intelligent character and jumping ability, makes the Dartmoor especially suitable for children.

The New Forest

Natives of the New Forest in Hampshire, these ponies were mentioned in the Domesday Book in 1085, since when much alien blood has been introduced into the forest. This has included most of the other native British breeds, also Arab and Thoroughbred; the result is that there is now a great variation in type and size. Forest ponies have had to learn to fend for themselves in poor conditions, and true forest ponies are very hardy. There are about 3,000 ponies in the forest today, but some inferior and poor stock can, unfortunately, be found there; most of the magnificent show specimens are now bred in private studs.

New Forest ponies usually stand between 12.2 and 14.2hh; the larger ponies are the ones most in demand as riding ponies. Like the Welsh (Section B), it is a

Left Dartmoor ponies have bred on the moor for hundreds of years. They are rounded up annually and the foals branded to identify their ownership, as can be seen on the grey pony.

Right A Welsh Mountain Pony (Section A); the most popular of all British native ponies, they have proved ideal childrens' riding ponies.

riding type of pony that is looked for, these being the only two classification of native ponies that are shown trimmed and plaited. Any colour other than skewbald or piebald are allowed, one of the many shades of bay being the most common. They usually have a good riding action, coming from a well-sloped shoulder with free, straight movement. The ponies in the forest are regularly rounded up for branding and tail marking, some of them being sold off each year at the Beaulieu Road Sales.

The Connemara

The only native breed of pony in Ireland, the Connemara, comes from the western area of the island, from whence it takes its name. The origin of these ponies is not known for certain, but they are a very old breed. Descended from the Celtic pony, it is believed to have Andalusian blood introduced from horses who swam ashore from wrecked Spanish Armada ships. Apart from that, the breed has remained pure, due to the inaccessible parts of the mountains where they breed. Some Arab and Thoroughbred blood was introduced during this century, to improve the quality, but only those ponies that are true to type are registered by the Society.

Connemara ponies are now bred in many countries, one problem being that they usually increase in size on the better pastures. They should be under 14hh, with a quality pony head, good length of rein, sloping shoulder and a good depth of girth. They may be grey, dun, bay, black or brown, and should be a sturdy, general-purpose type of riding pony. Crossed with a Thoroughbred they make excellent jumpers, one remarkable example being the internationally famous show jumper Dundrum, who only stood 14.3hh.

The Riding Pony

Although not a breed, this chapter would be incomplete without including the Riding Pony. A relatively recent development, produced mainly for the show ring, these ponies are exquisite miniature versions of the show hack. They have been developed basically by using small Thoroughbred stallions on native pony mares, notably the Welsh (Section B) and to a certain extent the Dartmoor. It is not the first cross that produces champions, but subsequent crosses, possibly introducing some Arab blood, which have produced some of the most outstanding ponies in the world. See page 107 above.

Pony breeding is a thriving hobby in Britain, with numerous studs and many individuals with their one extra special mare. Practically all horse shows now have classes for Riding Pony youngstock as well as the different height classes for the mature show ponies.

The Riding Pony is essentially an animal of quality, with that indefinable ingredient known as *presence*, which draws your attention to it. They must have good conformation, a fine intelligent head, good length of rein, well-sloping shoulder, depth of girth, good muscled quarters and well set-on tail. The limbs must be clean, with good bone, and the action should be free and straight coming from the shoulder and not from the knee. There are three main height limits in the show ring, not exceeding 12.2, 13.2 and 14.2hh.

There is also a demand for a rather heavier stamp of pony, more like a miniature hunter, for the working pony classes at shows. These ponies have to jump a course, and are judged on performance as well as conformation and manners. The heights for these ponies are rather different, being set not to exceed 13, 14 and 15hh.

Those Riding Ponies that do not reach the high standard required for the show ring make excellent mounts for children, for all riding activities and for hunting.

ICELAND

The Icelandic

Ponies were first taken to Iceland with the first settlers around AD 875. These settlers came from Norway, Orkney, Shetland and Ireland, bringing their household goods and livestock with them. The Icelandic ponies of today have descended from the different native breeds taken by these settlers, with some more blood introduced by settlers at later dates. Two main types have emerged, one rather heavier and larger that is used for draught and pack work, and a lighter type for riding.

Until about fifty years ago they were the only means of transport on the island. There used to be a good export trade of ponies to Britain to work in the mines, but with mechanization this trade died out. The harsh climatic conditions of Iceland are not suitable for cattle, and so ponies have always been bred for meat on the island. In the distant past they were also used for 'horse fighting' by Norse settlers, an unusual pastime in which fights to the death are described in old literature.

Today's ponies are extremely hardy; they are short and stocky, standing usually between 12–13hh although some larger ponies are to be found. They have very heavy thick manes and forelocks, with a large intelligent head set on a short thick neck. The most usual colours are grey and dun, although all other colours are seen; there are many shades of chestnuts often with flaxen manes and tails.

They make excellent trekking ponies, the most usual pace being a distinctive ambling gait known as the *tølt*, which covers a great deal of ground.

ITALY

The Avelignese

The Avelignese is a stocky packpony bred chiefly in the hilly areas around Tuscany and Venetia. They are used for light agricultural work and as pack animals in the Alps and Apennines. They are noted for being surefooted, and it is claimed that they get to know the tracks in their neighbourhood so well that they can travel at night almost as well as by day.

They are very similar to the Austrian Haflinger, to whom they are related, sharing the same ancestor, the now extinct Avellinum-Haflinger. Always a shade of chestnut with flaxen mane and tail or palomino, these attractive ponies stand 13.3–14.3hh, a little larger than the Haflinger. They are outstandingly muscular, with a wide chest, deep girth, strong quarters, short legs with plenty of bone and excellent feet. They are noted for their docile disposition and for living to a great age.

NORWAY

The Fjord

One of the oldest breeds, the Fjord or Westlands pony originated in West Norway from where it has spread throughout Scandinavia and into West Germany and Denmark, where it was much used for light agricultural work.

While most horses have been replaced by tractors, the Fjord pony has been kept on because it is so well suited for working in difficult terrain where motorized machinery can not be used. In fact there seem few jobs that this versatile pony is unable to do; from ploughing to hauling timber, carrying packs up difficult mountain passes and through rivers. It also makes an excellent riding and driving pony, with its docile and friendly nature.

The most distinctive feature of Fjord ponies is their colour; they are a *primitive* type with characteristic dun colouring and dark dorsal eel-stripe down the back. The mane and tail are thick and heavy, with the dark stripe running through the centre and pale hair on either side. The mane is normally clipped in a crescent, about 5–6in (13–15cm) long which gives the ponies the appearance of a very thick neck, whilst showing the two distinct hair colours. The legs are dark and occasionally zebra markings appear.

The pony-like head has wide-set intelligent eyes and is set on a short well-muscled neck. The Fjord pony is very surefooted, with short strong legs, standing 13–14.2hh. They are very hardy and tireless workers.

The Gudbrandsdal – Døle Gudbrandsdal

The famous old Norwegian breed named after the Gudbrandsdal Valley has great similarities with the Dales ponies of Britain and the Friesian horse from Holland.

Today this breed has almost been entirely merged with the Døle Trotter to form the breed known as the Døle Gudbrandsdal. These have spread throughout Scandinavia where they are used as a general utility and riding pony. Standing 14.2–15.2hh, they are always black, brown or bay. The head is neat and pony-like, the chest wide, the shoulders strong and the back rather long. They have a deep girth with powerful quarters and short strong legs with plenty of feather. The mane and tail are normally left long and thick.

Left A Norwegian Fjord pony mare and her twin foals. It is unusual for twins to be born to ponies, and this mare will need extra nourishment to keep in good condition herself while feeding them both.

Right Bay and grey New Forest ponies. These have run wild in the Forest for centuries, but heavy traffic is now a serious hazard, and the busiest roads are fenced, with underpasses for the ponies to cross to the other side.

Below right Connemara mare and foal in excellent condition on good, mixed summer pasture. The mare is the breed's original colour, a yellowish dun.

POLAND

The Hucul

Like the Konik, the other main breed of pony in Holland, the Hucul has probably descended directly from the Tarpan, dating back to the Stone Age. They come from the Huzulei district of the Carpathian Mountains, which was a part of Austria before World War I. There they have wandered the mountains for thousands of years, and are known locally as the Carpathian pony. In quite recent times Arab blood has been introduced to improve the breed, and selective breeding is now carried out at studs in Poland.

For centuries they were used as pack animals in difficult mountain country, carrying heavy burdens in all weather conditions. Today they are used mainly in harness and are the common work horse for thousands of farmers in the mountainous regions in the south of Poland.

Hucul ponies stand 12.1–13.1hh; they have the rather short head of the primitive breeds, are well muscled with a short neck and back, and a low-set tail. They may be any colour, the most common being brown, bay and dun.

The Konik

A native of Poland, the Konik, which means 'small horse', closely resembles the Tarpan from which it has descended. It thrives and works hard on a meagre diet, which makes it popular with the many small lowland farmers in Poland.

Like the Hucul there has been Arab blood introduced in comparatively recent times to improve the breed. It is now bred systematically at studs in Poland as well as by small farmers, and is in great demand in other countries as a work horse.

Rather larger than the Hucul, the Konik stands a little over 13hh, but has lost some of its pony characteristics and more resembles a horse. It is a tough and willing worker. The conformation is basically good, with a well-muscled neck and quarters, quite short back, rather upright shoulder and sturdy limbs. The colour is always one of the many shades of dun.

PORTUGAL AND SPAIN

The Garrano

The magnificent green pastures of the mountain valleys of the Portuguese provinces of Garrano do Minho and Traz dos Montes are the home of these excellent ponies. An infusion of Arab blood and selective breeding has produced a lightly-built pony with good conformation.

Standing only 10–12hh, these ponies are extremely hardy and very strong, being used for light agricultural work and timber hauling. They also make excellent riding ponies and in former times were used in traditional trotting races, which were run at a collected trot for which the ponies were specially bred and trained. Nearly always dark chestnut in colour, these ponies have a luxurious mane and tail.

The Sorraia

Found in the plains bordering the rivers Sor and Raia and their tributaries, the Sorraia is a native of both Spain and Portugal. It was possibly one of the first breeds to be domesticated, probably during Neolithic times. For hundreds of years it was the usual mount of the cowboys in the area and was also used for light agricultural work. It has retained the characteristics of both the Tarpan and Przewalski ponies, is extremely hardy and able to survive on poor vegetation, and withstand harsh climatic conditions.

Standing 12–13hh, they are usually dun in colour, though there are both greys and palominos. They often have the dark dorsal eel-stripe down the back, and zebra markings on the legs. The head is large, often with a convex profile, the ears long with black tips. The neck is long, the shoulder upright and the quarters poor with a low set tail. The breed has dwindled greatly over the years, only a few herds now remaining.

SWEDEN

The Gotland

This breed has existed on the Swedish island of Gotland in the Baltic Sea since the Stone Age. There is still a large herd running wild on the island in the forest of Lojsta, but today they are also bred on the mainland. Also known as the Russ or Skogsruss pony, this is the oldest breed in Scandinavia, probably having descended from the wild Tarpan.

Today they are used as children's riding ponies, making excellent jumpers, also for light agricultural work and for trotting races, for which some have been selectively bred.

Standing 12–12.2hh, their colours are bay, brown, black, chestnut, dun, palomino and grey. They are small rather light ponies, with a short well-muscled neck and good sloping shoulder. The back tends to be rather long, the quarters sloping to a low-set tail. The legs although light of bone are strong and well muscled, but the hindleg tends to be poor. The hooves are small but hard. These ponies are renowned for their speed and stamina, but though gentle, have a tendency to be obstinate.

3
PRINCIPLE BREEDS OF AFRICA, AMERICA, ASIA AND AUSTRALIA

A pretty liver chestnut Caspian stallion at a presentation held on Smith's Lawn, Windsor Great Park, which is also a famous polo ground. The Caspian, a miniature breed, was almost extinct, but is now increasing in popularity in Britain, where it is proving to make an ideal children's riding pony.

PRINCIPLE BREEDS OF AFRICA, AMERICA, ASIA AND AUSTRALIA

AFRICA

The Basuto

The Basuto pony is found in Namibia, Lesotho and South Africa, but in fact is not an indigenous African breed. Arabs and Barb horses were imported from Java in 1653; these were crossed, and Thoroughbreds were introduced to form the famous Cape Horse. These horses found their way into Basutoland (now Lesotho) during Zulu raids in the early nineteenth century, where they were crossed with the local scrub stock. The result was the establishment of the Basuto pony, which was used extensively during the Boer War.

Standing about 14.2hh, it is thick-set with short legs, longish back but with some quality in its head that comes from the Oriental blood in the past. It has very hard feet and is extremely surefooted, making it a very versatile pony, that may be ridden at speed over ground where other horses would be unsafe; it is also proving a useful polo pony.

AMERICA – the USA

The American Shetland

The American Shetland is now by far the most popular pony in the United States, with over forty thousand registered with the breed society. Developed in America by crossing imported Shetland ponies with Hackneys, the present day pony bears little resemblance to the original island ponies. Standing somewhat larger than their European cousins, the American Shetland must not exceed 11.2hh, although some are as small as only 7hh. Much more refined, with an Oriental look, these ponies have a neat small head, often slightly dished, set on an elegant neck with longer, finer legs than their ancestors. Whilst the mane and tail still grow quite thick, the coat is much finer and silkier, also helping to give a sleeker, trimmer appearance.

Bred throughout the United States, the sums demanded for these ponies are far from small, the most remarkable figures, into tens of thousands of dollars, being raised at auction sales for good stock.

Often kept as pets as well as children's ponies, numerous competitive sports are arranged for Shetlands. Hunter types are shown over a course of 2ft (60cm) jumps, saddle types are shown copying the horse breeds, prancing through the different gaits with exaggerated action. Both in these classes and the harness classes the ponies have their tails nicked, a controversial practice, to give an artificially high tail carriage. One of the latest crazes is to race American Shetlands in a lightweight racing sulky, when children can get the real feel of the racetrack without the expense or danger of the real thing.

The Chincoteague

These ponies inhabit the small islands of Chincoteague and Assateague off the coast of Virginia. Their origin is obscure, but they may well have been the survivors of shipwrecks during the Spanish colonization wars in the sixteenth and seventeenth centuries. The island vegetation is very poor and there is no shelter from the Atlantic storms, with the possible result that these ponies have lost much of their size, now standing less than 12hh, whilst still retaining an appearance more like a horse. Recent introduction of Arab blood has improved their quality, but they still appear rather poor specimens. Many of them are piebald or skewbald with a poor coat. There is an annual round-up when the ponies are branded and offered for sale, often the best being sold, thus leaving the poorer specimens to run wild again and breed.

The Pony of the Americas

This very recent breed results from an experiment in 1956 when a Shetland stallion was crossed on to an Appaloosa mare. The pleasing consequence was the basis of this new breed which has fulfilled a useful need throughout America, producing a useful child's pony with plenty of substance.

To qualify for registration in the Stud Book, the ponies must be examined by a veterinary or club inspector at the age of three. They must be one of the six accepted Appaloosa colours and measure between 11.2 and 13hh. The head should be small with a dished profile and Araby look; the ears small, eyes large, shoulder sloping, chest wide, body deep. The quarters must be well muscled, the tail set on high, the legs short with plenty of bone. These ponies have proved successful in many sports, including jumping, trail riding and racing.

CANADA

The Sable Island

Ponies were first introduced to the Sable Islands in the early eighteenth century. These sand-banks, about 25 miles (40km) long and 200 miles (320km) off the coast of Nova Scotia, afford little in the way of food or shelter. The ponies, numbering about three hundred, run wild, living off the dune or scrub grasses. Standing about 14hh, these scrub ponies may be any colour, although chestnut predominates. They are lightly built, but very tough and hardy; some are used in harness and under saddle by the lighthouse keepers on the island.

MEXICO

The Galiceno

This breed has developed with little help from man. It takes its name from Galicia in north-west Spain, the area from which the original Spanish horses were taken by Hernando Cortes, the conqueror of Mexico, in 1519 and from which they are believed to have descended. A native of Mexico, these ponies have spread throughout America in the last twenty years, where they have proved intelligent, and versatile and are used in many competitions.

Standing only 12–13.2hh, they may be bay, black, dun, grey or chestnut. They have a fine head, upright shoulder and short back. They tend to be narrow-chested and rather light of bone, having a characteristic natural running walk.

SOUTH AMERICA

The Criollo

Horses were first taken to America by Columbus in 1493, but of more importance to South America were the Andalusian horses shipped there in 1535 by Don Pedro Mendozo. These horses later escaped and bred freely on the plains, forming enormous herds. They had to be tough to survive, coping with severe winters and long droughts in the summers. Some of these were captured by the settlers and were given the name *Criollos*; they were used for carrying packs and their owners over very rough country through mountains, and for long distances on the plains and developed a reputation for being tough and hardy with powers of endurance.

The Criollo is used throughout South America (Argentina, Brazil, Chile, Venezuela and Peru) as a general stock pony. The height and type varies according to the area, but they are all the same basic stamp. Standing between 13.2 and 15hh, they are sturdy, compact animals with a short broad head, wide between the eyes. The neck and quarters are muscular and well developed, the back short and the chest wide. The legs are short with good bone, the feet hard. Dun is the most usual colour, with a dark dorsal stripe, and zebra markings on the legs, often with some white on the head and legs. Other colours include bay, roan, chestnut, grey, palomino, black, skewbald and piebald.

The Falabella

This miniature breed has been developed by the Falabella family over the last hundred years at their ranch outside Buenos Aires, Argentina. Based on Shetland stock, crossed with small Thoroughbreds, and then in-breeding of the smallest animals, the Falabella can truly claim to be the smallest breed in the world, standing under 7.2hh. Unfortunately no records were kept, and in the process the toughness and hardiness of the Shetland has been lost. The coat is long and silky, but without the dense undercoat of the Shetland. Delightfully pretty and well-proportioned, these ponies are not suitable for riding but are kept mainly as pets and for use in harness, especially in North America. All colours are to be found but Appaloosa-marked ponies are the most popular; that is, brown spots on white coats, or the reverse.

INDIA

The Bhutia and the Spiti

Several different breeds developed in the north of India, all based on the Mongolian pony. The Bhutia and the Spiti are two similar breeds from the Himalayan mountain regions, used mainly as packponies. Both are hardy, surefooted with plenty of stamina and able to live on very little food. They are quite sturdy, with plenty of bone and well-muscled quarters. The Bhutia stands between 13 and 13.2hh and is usually grey in colour, while the Spiti is smaller, usually only about 12hh. They both tend to be rather temperamental.

The Kathiawari and the Marwari

Both these breeds are very alike, having descended from the local breeds being crossed with Arabs. They are generally of poor conformation, being narrow and light of bone, with weak necks and quarters. The ears curl inwards, nearly meeting at the top, showing the Arab influence. The tail is low-set, the legs short of muscle and with sickle hocks. They are, however, very tough, have lots of stamina and are able to survive on very little food. Like the other Indian breeds, they tend to be bad tempered. They stand between 12 and 13.2hh.

INDONESIA

Many of the islands in Indonesia have their own variety of pony which plays an important part in the life and economy of the islands. These have mainly descended from the Mongolian and Tarpan ponies of Central Asia imported thousands of years ago. Arab blood has been used to improve many of these native ponies, particularly on the islands of Sumatra where the Batak has an added touch of elegance. A general purpose animal standing 12–13hh, it can be any colour, and is often shipped to the other islands to improve the quality of their stock.

On the island of Bali the ponies resemble the Mongolian pony, being dun in colour with an upright mane and dark dorsal eel-stripe down the centre of the back. Of a similar height, 12–13hh they are most commonly used as pack ponies.

The ponies in Java are mostly used to pull two-wheeled vehicles known as sados, which are normally heavily laden, and are used as taxis on the island. These ponies are tough and hardy in spite of being light of bone, generally with poor conformation; long backs and legs, and weak necks and quarters. They appear very willing and apparently tireless.

The Sandalwood pony is named after the chief export on the islands of Sumba and Sumbawa. Arab blood has influenced these ponies and shows in the head, the hard legs, deep girth and fine coat. The best of these ponies are raced over distances of $2\frac{1}{2}$–3 miles (4–5km) although they only stand about 12.2hh. They are ridden bareback with a bitless plaited leather bridle with a hard nosepiece similar to those used 4,000 years ago in Central Asia. They are also used in lance-throwing, the national sport of Indonesia, and in 'dancing' competitions. The ponies have bells attached to their knees; they are ridden bareback by young boys while a trainer directs the various movements on the end of a lunge line and the ponies dance in time to the beat of the tom-toms.

The ponies on the island of Timor are the smallest of the Indonesian breeds, standing only 11–12hh. They are exceptionally strong and agile and are used as cowponies. They are also very intelligent, surefooted yet docile; many are exported to Australia as they make excellent children's riding ponies. They have a small head, short back and good strong legs and feet, the usual colours being black, bay or brown.

IRAN

The Caspian

It was thought for over 1,000 years that the miniature horses, used for ceremonial purposes from the fifth century BC until the seventh century AD, were extinct. However, in 1965 a few were found around the shores of the Caspian Sea, some of them being used for pulling carts. Since then great interest has been shown in them, with a Caspian pony society being formed in Britain to promote the breed. Research is still being carried out in an attempt to prove beyond doubt that these miniature horses have indeed descended from those used by the Mesopotamians two thousand years ago. See page 34.

The Caspian pony stands between 10 and 12hh. They may be grey, bay, brown or chestnut in colour, bay being the predominant colour. They have a small, Arab-like head, with large wide set eyes. The back is short, the chest narrow and the legs very fine. The hindleg tends to be poor, but despite this they have proved to have remarkable jumping ability, which combined with their surefootedness make them excellent childrens' riding ponies. They are attractive, elegant little ponies.

USSR

The Kazakh

These are an ancient breed of pony, originally bred in the Kazakhstan region, and they resemble the Mongolian horses of China. They are an exceptionally hardy breed, capable of foraging for themselves in extremes of climatic conditions, either thick snow or in the desert. They stand between 12.2–13.2hh, but when crossed with the Don or the Akhal-Teke the result is often a good size, and they have produced very good cavalry mounts. Their main use is as cowponies for the local herdsmen, they have hard limbs and feet and make strong willing mounts. The mares are often used to produce milk which is made into a drink called 'kumiss', best described as a light alcoholic type of yoghurt; many of the youngsters are also fattened for meat. The most usual colours are grey, bay, chestnut or black.

The Viatka

This pony is a native of the Baltic States and is bred around the Viatka and Obva rivers. They stand between 13–14hh and have proved very good as harness horses, both for light farm work but principally for pulling the troika (three-horse) sledges. They have a peculiar trotting gait which is well suited to snowbound roads and tracks.

Viatka ponies have rather large heads, typical of the primitive breeds; the ears and lower jaw are large, but frequently the profile is slightly concave at the forehead. The neck and quarters are well-muscled, the back short with a good depth through the girth. The legs tend to be short and strong, the forelegs set wide apart, although the hindlegs are inclined to be sickle hocked. The most common colours are duns, roans, and mousey greys, usually with a dark dorsal stripe.

The Yakut

This is a remarkable breed, whose territory includes some of the coldest areas in the northern hemisphere, extending far beyond the polar circle; the average winter temperature being minus 40–50°C. Yakut ponies have to dig out their food from under deep snow in winter and be able to withstand the attacks of millions of blood-sucking insects in the brief summer.

They are very adaptable animals, being used as packponies, in harness and under saddle. They also provide both milk and meat, and are raced on festive occasions. Standing between 12 and 14hh, these remarkably tough ponies have developed an exceptionally long, thick coat which may be 3–4 inches (8–10cms) long and which is usually one of the shades of grey, often with dark patterning on the shoulders.

AUSTRALASIA

The Australian Pony

There were no horses or ponies in Australia until they were taken there about 200 years ago. Since then a variety of ponies have been imported, and it is from a mixture of these that the Australian pony has derived.

The Welsh Mountain Pony is the foundation, with mixtures of Arab, Thoroughbred, Timor and Shetland. The height varies between 12 and 14 hands producing a cobby type of child's riding pony that is intelligent, hardy and sound. Any whole colours are permitted, grey and chestnut being predominant.

4
LEARNING TO RIDE

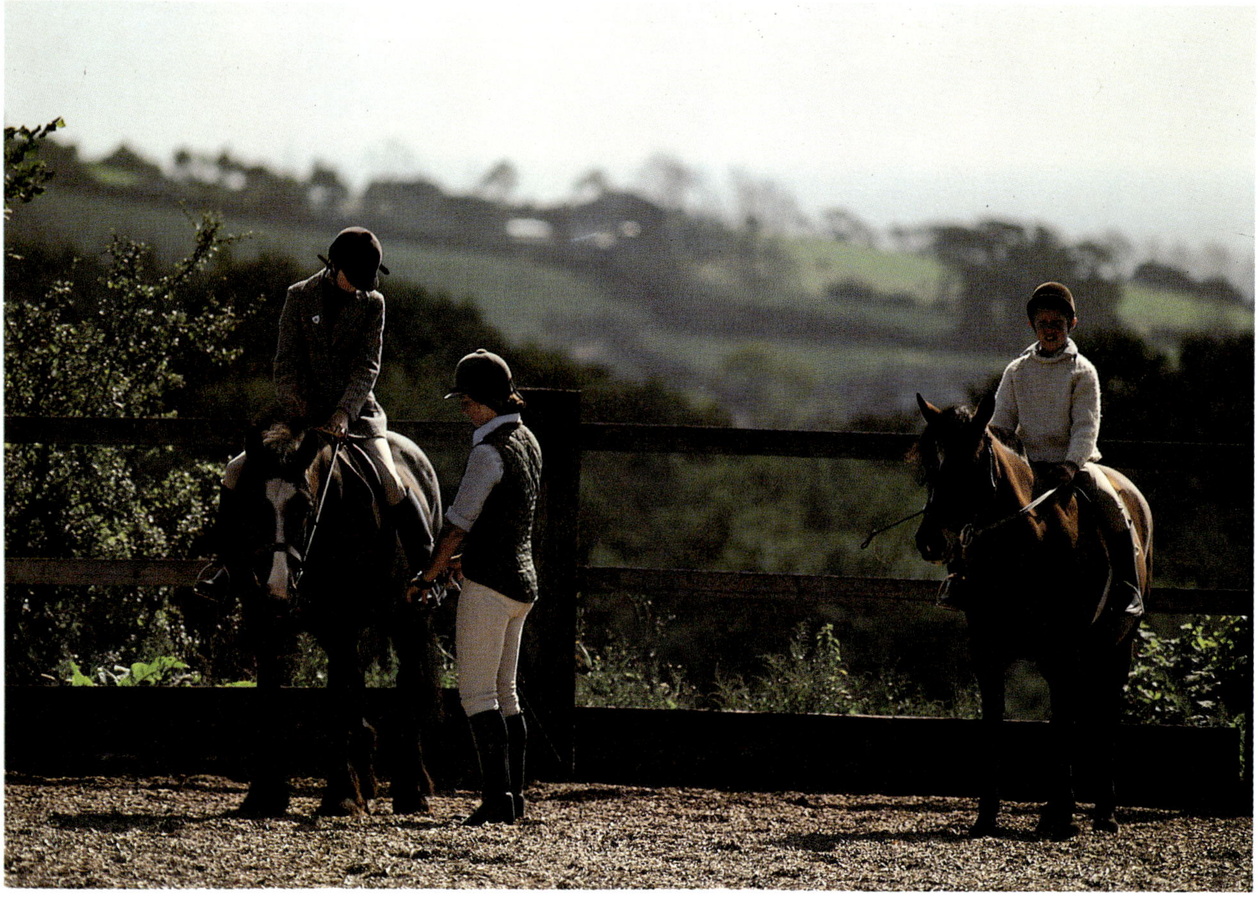

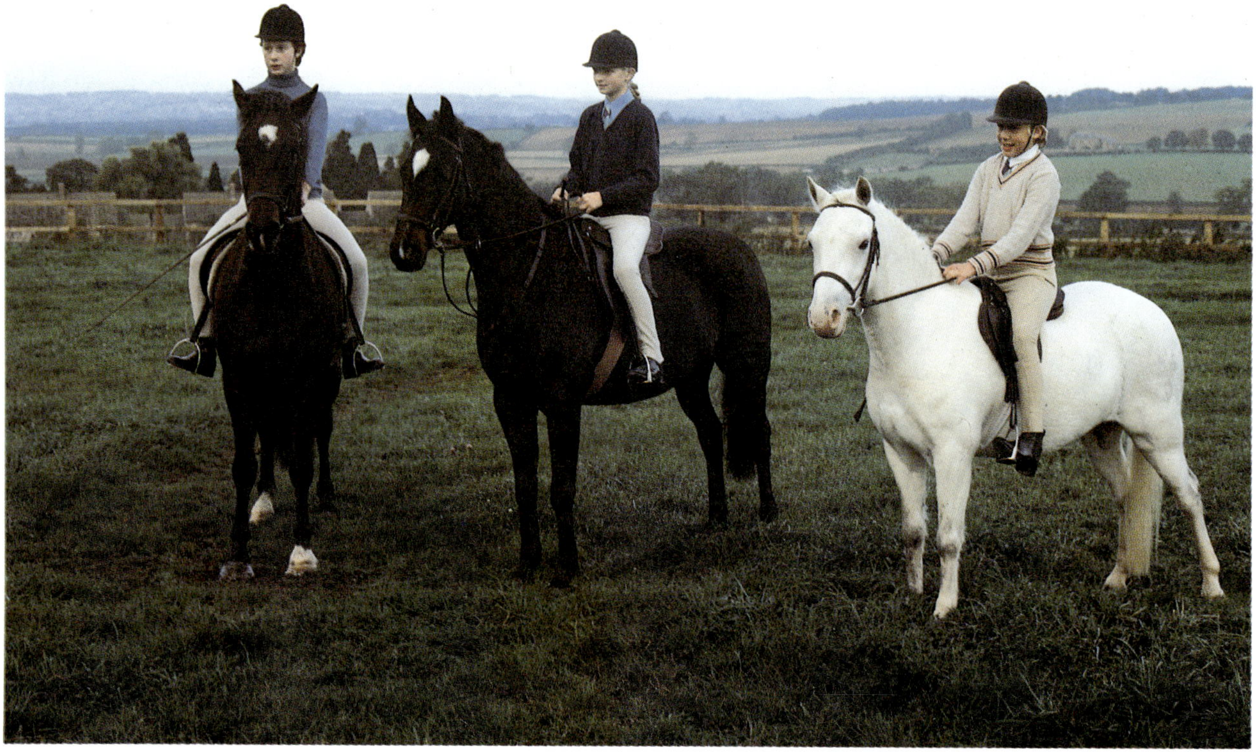

LEARNING TO RIDE

Learning to ride a pony can not, of course be taught from books or a blackboard, but an understanding of the requirements before attempting to put them into practice can be a great help. In this chapter there is only room for the basic essentials to be discussed; many volumes have been written and will continue to be written on the finer details of advanced equitation.

If you want to learn to ride, then it is very important that you are taught correctly. Go to a good riding school; a list of approved ones can be obtained from The British Horse Society or from the Association of British Riding Schools (see Address list). Don't think that after a few lessons you will be able to cope with your own pony; you will need to establish a good seat and learn a great deal about the care of ponies before you contemplate that.

There are, today, more opportunities for people to learn to ride than ever before. No longer is it a sport only for the wealthy landed gentry; indeed many people living in urban areas not only learn to ride but own their own ponies. Unfortunately, it is also a fact that many people acquire a pony without enough knowledge or experience to cope with it correctly. The care of horses and ponies used to be left to grooms, who had a thorough grounding, learned by working under a head groom, in their management. Today, many 'do-it-yourself' owners are woefully lacking in knowledge.

To become a good horseman you will not only have to establish a good independent seat, and be able to apply the aids correctly, but you will also have to study the theory of riding. This way you will progress to the second stage of equitation, when you will execute some more advanced movements on a trained horse or pony. Later you will be able to teach a youngster the basic schooling before you both should advance to greater things.

Riding clothes

Over the years, riding clothes have developed to be comfortable, practical and safe. A riding hat is essential at all times; few falls are anticipated, and someone can just as easily crack their skull from a fall walking down a country lane, as from jumping cross-country at speed. It should have a chinstrap. Breeches or jodhpurs provide a comfortable fit and protect the legs from chaffing. These are now mostly of stretchy manmade fibre, easily washable and quick-drying.

Footwear is also of utmost importance. Shoes with high heels, buckles or fancy designs can be dangerous. Proper jodhpur boots or long riding boots are the best footwear; but sensible walking shoes with leather soles and flat heels are alright. There are also on the market many makes of long rubber riding boots; provided these are properly made and fitted they are quite adequate for everyday riding. Regrettably one so often sees children wearing rubber riding boots that are either too big, or are very baggy round the top. These not only look untidy but are dangerous; do be careful to find a boot that has a good solid heel and fits both the foot and the leg correctly.

When riding in a school or out hacking, a shirt with or without a pullover is

Above left Here the instructor is teaching the pupil the correct position of the leg and foot in the stirrup.

Left A group of riders correctly dressed at the start of their lesson, in jodhpurs, jodhpur boots, hard hats and neat, quiet-coloured jumpers. The grey pony has an eggbutt snaffle bit and cavesson noseband (the most usual sort of bridle). The brown ponies both have a white star and snip.

quite adequate; sleeves should be worn to protect arms and elbows in the event of a fall. If you go to a function with your pony then a collar and tie and a proper hacking jacket will be necessary. The jacket should have a full skirt and be divided at the back so that it will fall around the saddle and not come between the rider's seat and the saddle.

Always wear gloves; they protect your fingers from blisters and help prevent the reins slipping. Riding without them at a function or competition is incorrect, and in the winter you will be more than grateful to keep your hands warm.

Riding on roads

After you have learnt to ride in a school and can manage a pony, you will probably ride on the roads at some stage. It is very important that you should know the riding Highway Code and be a responsible road user.

Motorists do not always show the consideration they should for riders, but riders should always be considerate to other road users. When a motorist slows down, acknowledge this by raising a hand, or with a smile and a nod. When riding in groups, never ride more than two abreast, and make sure that you do not block the road if waiting in a group. You can buy safety tabards and armbands in 'dayglo' material to make yourself more visible to drivers on the roads. One London riding school equips all its pupils with them.

When going through a gate, never leave the last person alone to shut the gate, as his pony will fuss and make the task difficult. Politeness and good manners have always been associated with good horsemanship, as has correct turnout and dress.

Today horses and ponies are used for many and varied purposes; for sports such as hacking, hunting, racing, showjumping, polo and dressage. They are also used as a means of transport by cavalry soldiers, mounted policemen and cowboys. We ask them to carry us for a wide range of activities in which different duties are required of them. This has led to the development of many different styles of riding, all of which are correct for their own purpose. It would not be practical for a cowboy, in the saddle for maybe up to twelve hours, to try and ride like a jockey, who will only be on the horse's back for a few minutes of the race. There are, however, several basic requirements common to all forms of riding, so these we will discuss in some detail.

Balance

The first essential of riding is balance. In the wild a pony is a well-balanced animal, capable of moving gracefully and swiftly in all his natural paces. The moment a weight is placed on him it upsets this natural balance, and he has to learn to adjust to moving in balance with this additional encumbrance. The rider can assist the pony a great deal by placing the weight in the place where he finds it easiest to carry. You know yourself that when you carry a knapsack on your back, if it is too low or unevenly loaded it is much more difficult to carry. Likewise with a pony; if the weight is too far back or lop-sided then it will make his task less easy.

The strongest part of the pony's spine, and that most capable of carrying a load, is the part of the back immediately behind the withers. Here the rib-cage completely encases the abdomen, the ribs joining underneath onto the sternum, or breast bone.

When a young pony is first mounted, the additional weight upsets his own balance, the weight is too far forward and he will *be on his forehand*. As he exercises and is schooled, the muscles of the back and hindlegs will develop and slowly he will learn to adjust to carrying the additional load.

A well-balanced rider will be an easier load for him to carry. We must therefore learn to ride *in balance* at all times, both uphill and downhill and through all increases and decreases of pace. Some people will find it much easier to stay *in balance* than others, just as some people learn to ski or swim more easily than others.

Aids

The second essential to all forms of riding is a system of communication from rider to pony. Without this, riding is not only no pleasure for either party, but is also dangerous. The system used to communicate is known as the *aids*. The rider gives the aids to the pony to tell him what he wants him to do. The aids can be divided into natural aids; the voice, weight, legs and hands; and the artificial aids which includes whips, spurs and martingales. The important thing about the aids is that they should be applied quickly and effectively; this can only be done by a rider who sits correctly and quietly in the saddle. See page 49 for a fuller description.

The seat

Learning to ride a pony is not as simple as learning to ride a bicycle; but the art, once correctly learnt, can be enormously rewarding. Beginners must be prepared to take the time and tuition necessary to establish a good position before they launch off on their own.

Although there are many ways to ride that are all correct for their own particular field, varying from the flat-race jockey with ultra short stirrups, to the cowboy who rides with his legs at full stretch, we will base our teachng on the classical style. This is the style used by the Spanish Riding School in Vienna, the last truly great school of advanced equitation.

The beginner should be taught on a mannerly and well-schooled pony. Trying to learn on a young *green* (inexperienced) pony is a certain recipe for disaster for both parties.

The rider must learn to develop a firm and independent seat in the saddle. Without this he will be unable to give the correct aids to the pony, resulting in confusion and resistance on the part of the pony. To help the rider sit in the correct position it is essential to have a saddle with a good central position that allows him to sit deep into his pony.

If you are buying a saddle, get some expert help to see that it not only fits the pony correctly, but that the deepest part is well forward and that it has a narrow *waist*. The old type of hunting saddle that slopes back towards the *cantle* will ensure that the poor rider slides backwards and spends most of his efforts trying to sit further forward in the saddle!

To achieve a good seat the rider must sit in the lowest part of the saddle with the crotch well forward. The weight should be placed equally on both seat bones, not on the fleshy part of the buttocks. Some of the weight will go into the thighs which should lie softly against the saddle. The knees should be relaxed so that the lower leg will hang around the pony's sides in a relaxed way, the inside of the calf keeping a steady contact.

The length of the stirrup leathers is vital and depends on the length and shape of the rider's thigh. Leathers that are too long will cause a rider to tip forward and become unbalanced reaching for the stirrups. Too short a leather will cramp the rider's knee and will cause the seat to be pushed too far back in the saddle.

Provided the saddle is correctly proportioned, the stirrup leathers should hang vertically when the ball of the foot is placed in the stirrup. The ankle acts as a buffer and must not therefore be locked; the heel should be a little lower than the toe, with the ankle relaxed so that it will give with each stride.

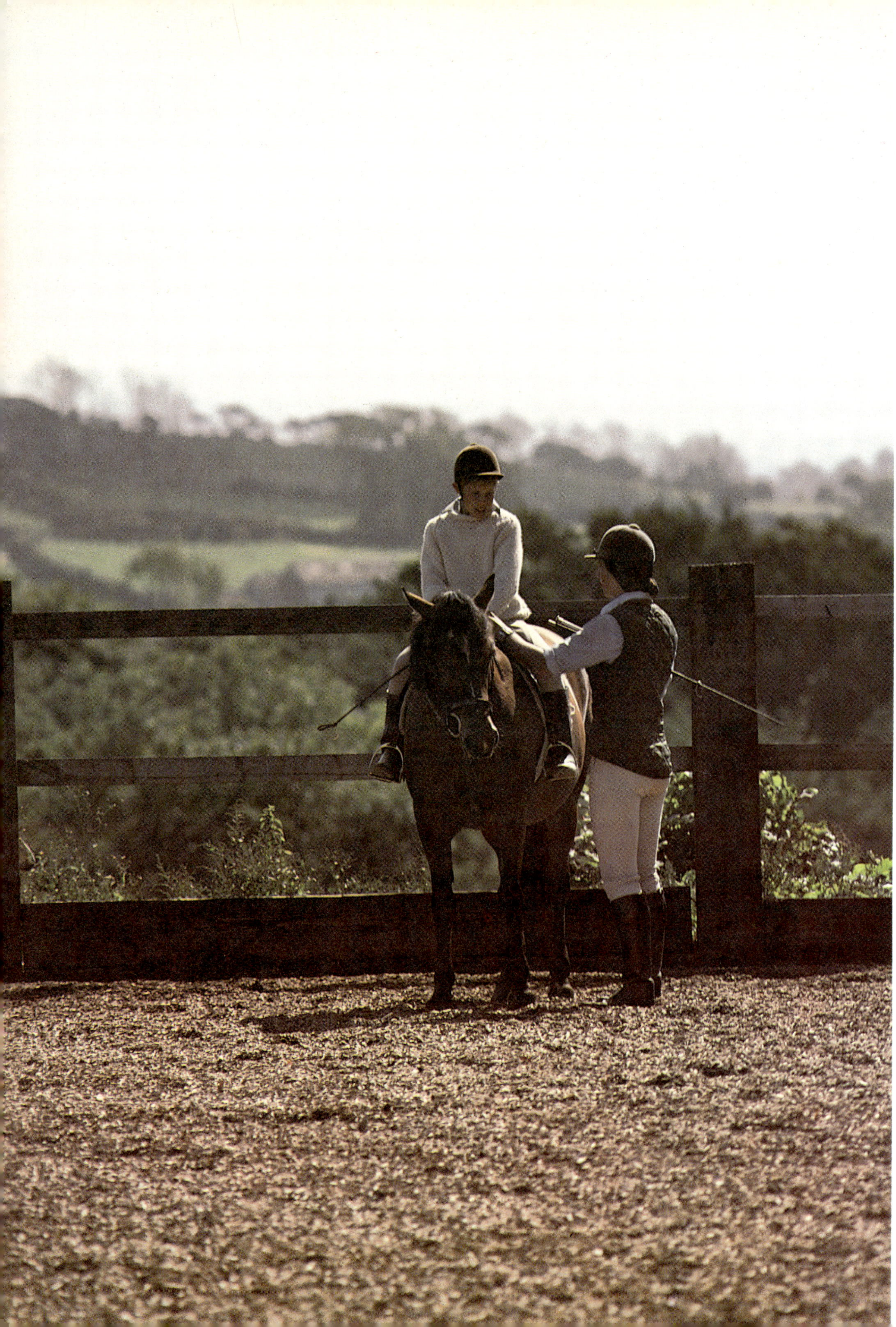

Left The instructor is teaching this beginner to hold his reins correctly: between the third and little fingers, fingers curled towards the inside and thumbs up uppermost.

Right These young riders are having a lesson in an enclosed manège, which is a great help for both pupils and instructor for taking early lessons. The leading pony is piebald.

Below Loosening-up exercises at the beginning of a lesson. The leading rider is really stretching her arm up well but whilst doing so has lifted her heel.

Below right When coming down a slope the rider must incline his weight forward to allow the pony to use his hindquarters correctly.

For the rider to be in balance, his body must be upright, with his hips and shoulders parallel to the pony's shoulders. He should feel the back of his neck in the back of his collar and point his nose between his pony's ears. The head is most important to both balance and suppleness; if it is carried to one side or pushed forward it will upset his balance and cause him to stiffen.

Many beginners are told to grip, but in fact this is a grave fault and will lead to all kinds of problems. The rider will stiffen the knee, turn his toe out and grip with the back of the calf, thus forcing himself out of the saddle like a cork out of a bottle. Grip is a technique which can be acquired as the rider becomes more proficient. It will be used later in his training when he learns to jump cross-country at speed.

As a rider adjusts to sitting in the saddle he will gradually sit deeper. His back and loins should never get rounded, as this will stiffen the body. He should allow his tummy to fall forward and lift his chest. The motto *ride tall* is a very good one for the beginner. The rider who sits correctly and is supple will be in balance and harmony with his pony. He will look elegant and will make a pleasing picture to the eye.

The hands

No rider will become a good horseman without having good hands. It is true that until a rider has established a firm and independent seat, he will not be able to achieve good hands, but nevertheless it is possible to teach the beginner to put his arms and hands in a position from which he will develop them. Suppleness of the elbows, wrists and fingers is essential; but first let us discuss the correct position.

The upper arm should hang naturally from the shoulder, the rein should be of sufficient length that the elbow never goes behind the hip, as this will stiffen the whole body. The elbow must be kept soft and relaxed, the wrist nearly straight. Beginners are best with only one rein to hold; this is placed between the third and little fingers of the hand, the fingers curled towards the inside and the thumbs uppermost.

As a pony walks forward his head moves with each step. The rider should keep a light contact with his mouth; his hands must learn to follow the movement of every step. He should try to keep a straight line from his elbow, through his fingers, down the rein to the bit. His hands should be at least the width of the bit apart and a little way above the withers.

The rider must also learn to follow the movement of the pony with his own body. Each pace has a different rhythm and he must learn to conform to each pace, keeping his body relaxed and supple.

With the help of a good instructor, on a well-schooled and balanced pony, the beginner should soon get the feel of moving with the pony, rather than in opposition to him. By degrees he will attain the correct position in the saddle; he must then practise exercises to develop his natural balance and muscles to keep him there. A competent horseman will appear at ease in the saddle, but at the same time be able to give the aids quietly, efficiently and independently.

Exercises

To work towards this end, the rider should practise a number of exercises, to help him attain true balance without the support of the reins. Five minutes spent on exercises at the beginning of every ride will help enormously. They are designed to relax both horse and rider, and help the rider to attain a deeper seat.

Never attempt to do exercises loose in a field unless the pony is held by someone or on the lunge. The following exercises will be of great benefit to the rider if done at the beginning of the lesson. They should at first be done at the halt without stirrups, then later at the walk on the lunge, finally at a trot on the lunge.

1) Holding the pommel lightly with two fingers of each hand, the rider lifts both thighs slightly from the saddle with the knees bent. Keeping the back upright, the rider should feel the weight of his body on his seat bones. Repeat this exercise six times.

2) Stretching down and back with his knees, the rider stretches his back upwards and looks up at the roof or sky; then he relaxes. Repeat this six times.

3) Bringing his knees back to a more natural position in the saddle, the rider circles his feet outwards to supple the ankles.

4) Keeping his lower legs still and close to the horse's sides, the rider practises moving the hands independently. Move one to the right, one upwards then one forwards and one downwards and so forth.

5) The rider puts first one hand behind the neck and forces the elbow backwards and forwards, then he repeats it with the other hand. Repeat six times each hand.

6) The rider holds the back of the saddle with both hands, palms facing forward, then pushes down with the hands, this forces the chest forwards and arches the back.

The natural reflex to contract the muscles must be overcome. These exercises aimed at extending the muscles, will also improve the rider's balance and give him confidence at the same time.

Riding without stirrups can be of benefit to all riders if it is done in small doses. Riding for too long without stirrups will give the rider tired and aching muscles and he will adopt an incorrect position to alleviate the aching. The object is to encourage a deeper seat, to improve balance, to supple the body and limbs and encourage them to work independently of each other. The legs should be relaxed and lie quietly against the sides of the pony; they should never grip as this will cause the body to stiffen and defeat the object of the exercises.

The aids

The *aids* as they are termed, are the signals the rider uses to convey his intentions to the pony, and the means at his disposal for conveying these signals. We have already said that there are both natural and artificial aids.

When a pony is lunged, the trainer will use a cavesson, a whip and his voice. The combined use of these, instantly rewarded when the pony obeys, will teach him to answer to the correct aids.

When the pony is ridden he will be trained to answer the other aids, particularly those of the legs and hands. The rider must be taught to give these aids correctly, and also to know the effect that they have on the pony.

The Voice is the first aid that a young pony will become accustomed to when he begins to be led as a foal; it will also be used when he is lunged. It can also be used to great effect, if used in a soothing manner, to quieten a pony when he gets excited. It should not be used in competitions and its use is penalized in dressage tests.

The Weight of the body, applied through the seat, plays an important part in influencing the pony. In more advanced training the correct distribution of the rider's weight is of the utmost importance. The beginner will be unable to apply the correct aids unless his weight is in the right place; and so he should be encouraged to sit square and still, with his weight evenly distributed on both seat bones, moving in harmony with his pony.

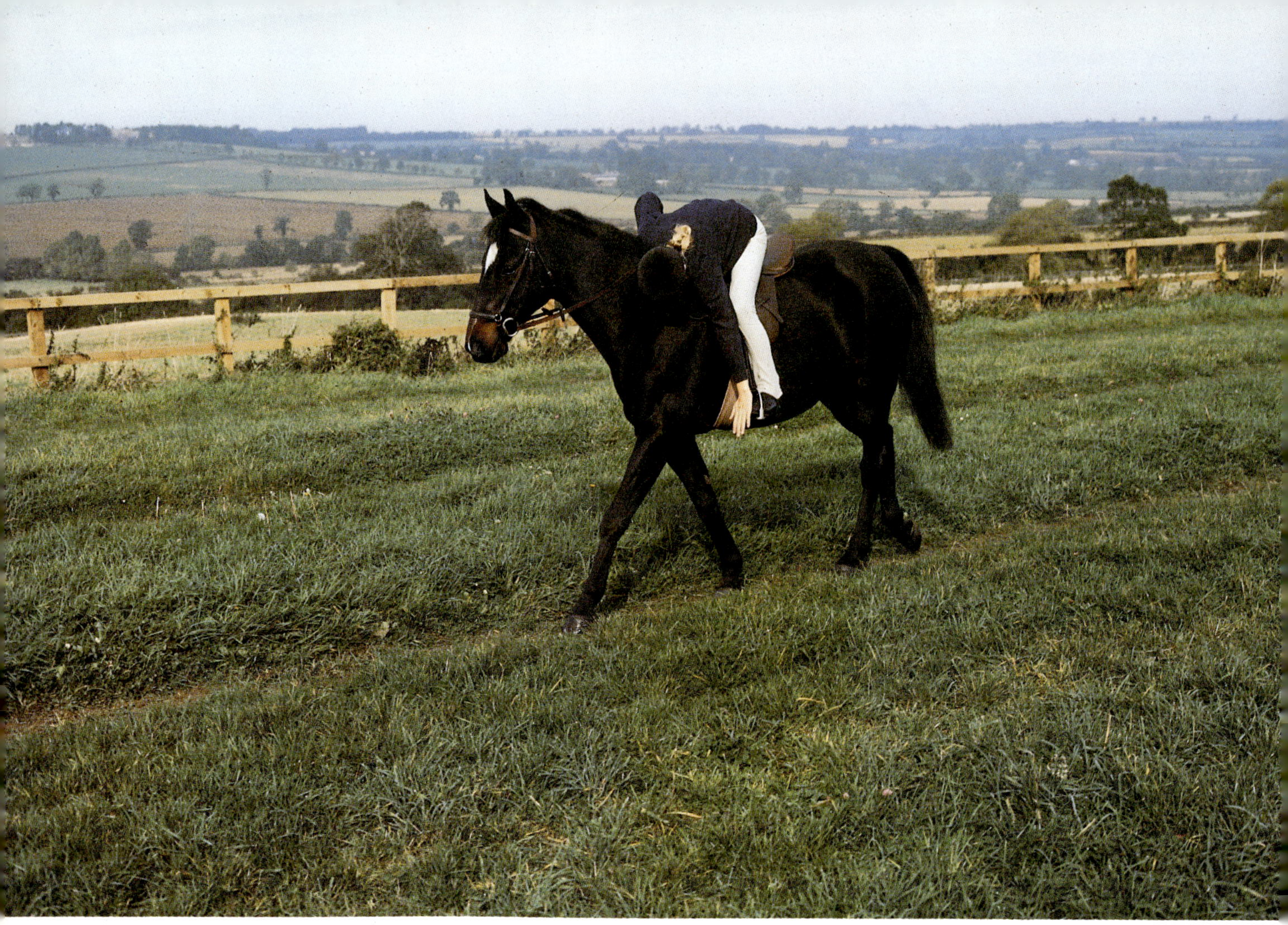

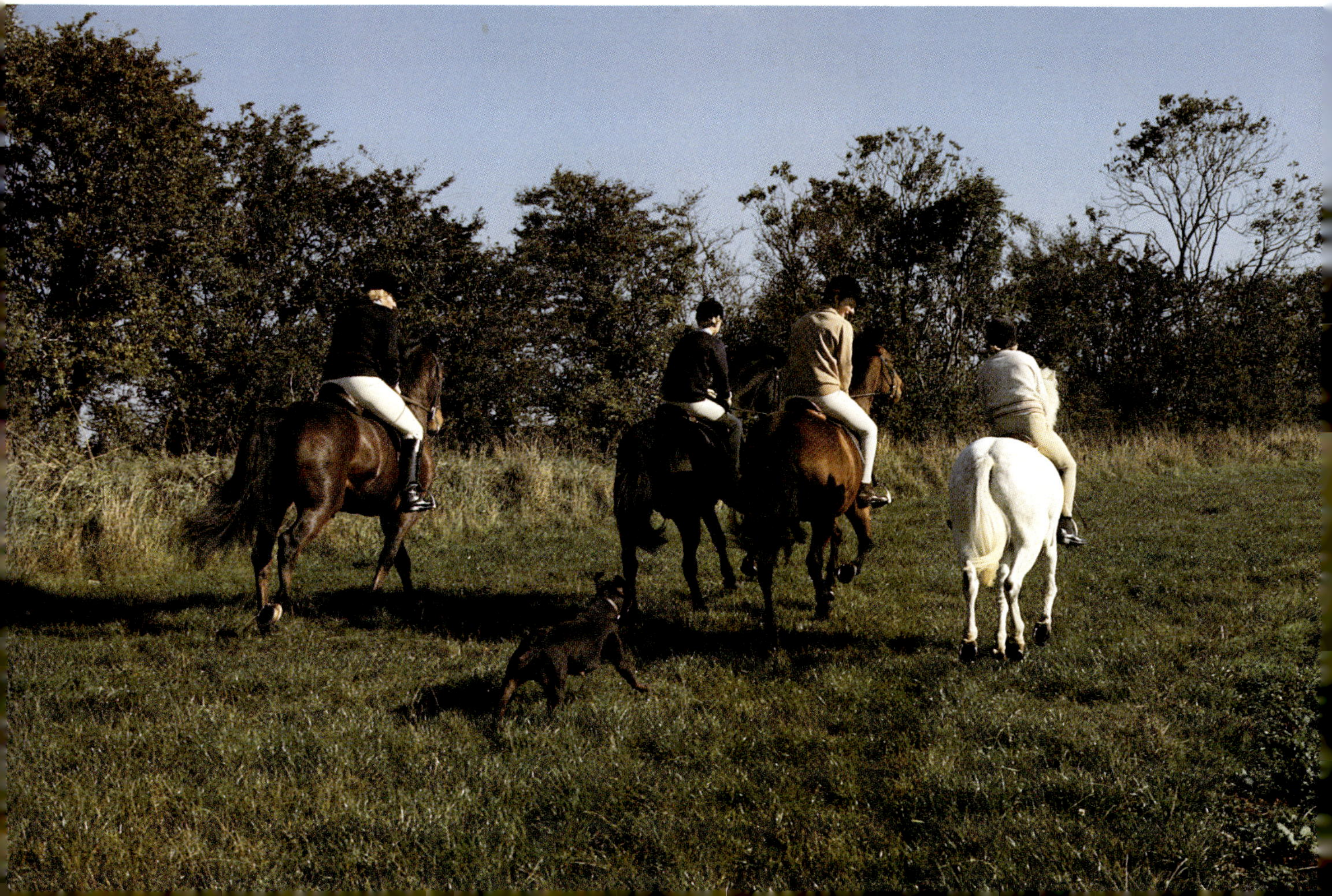

The Legs have two important functions, both of which the beginner can practise from the outset. Firstly, they create and maintain impulsion. The lower leg should at all times maintain a light contact with the pony's sides; an aid is given by applying pressure close to the girth. The aid should be the minimum necessary to produce the desired result; a continual kicking of the pony's sides will only deaden this sensitive area and become totally useless. A well-schooled pony will move forward to the slightest squeeze.

The legs are also used to guide and control the hindquarters. By using one leg with more force behind the girth, the hindquarters of a trained pony can be moved laterally, that is, sideways.

The Hands are the last but by no means the least of the natural aids at our disposal. We have already said that good hands are essential to a competent horseman, also that a firm and independent seat is necessary.

The beginner should be taught to keep his hands passive, moving with the movement of the pony's head. The hands must never pull; the pony, after all, is much stronger and will always win in a battle of sheer strength. The hands should resist to decrease pace or indicate direction; they must also yield to increase pace or after completing a downward transition (see page 52 and 55).

It is most important that a rider is taught to develop the correct reflexes, so that he can sit in a position of resistance when necessary. Without the correct length of rein he will be unbalanced and fall into the trap so commonly seen, of hauling on the reins. The reins themselves are important; they should be broad and non-slip, but also supple, as stiff reins will create insensitive fingers. A mild snaffle bit is the best to start with, although later some other bit may be more suitable. See page 79.

Harmony of the aids   At first the rider must be taught to yield with his hands when asking for a forward movement with his legs. This does not mean letting the reins hang in loops; he should always maintain a light elastic contact, with supple fingers and wrists and a soft elbow.

By degrees the rider will learn to use the different aids in conjunction with each other. He must also learn to get the correct balance between the aids. Too often a rider will use much more hand than leg; a rider with *busy* hands, that are always fiddling with his pony's mouth, will have bad hands.

As a rider develops his seat and progresses in his training, he will learn to apply the aids more efficiently. The aids must always be clear and definite. With a young pony they will probably have to be rather exaggerated. As the training of the pony progresses they will become more delicate, until with the trained animal they will be virtually unnoticeable to the onlooker.

So with the rider; at first his aids will be somewhat clumsy and exaggerated. As he acquires a greater control of his muscles he will be able to give neater, more precise aids. The aids should always be the lightest possible to get the best results.

The aids and transitions   As we have said, the legs create and maintain the impulsion; the hands, through the reins, have to control and direct that impulsion. The change from one pace to another is known as a transition. Increases of pace are known as upward transitions, while decreases of pace are called downward transitions.

Let us begin with the simplest of all transitions, that from a halt to a walk. The rider should just feel his pony's mouth with a light contact on the reins. He then closes his legs and squeezes the pony's sides just behind the girth; at the same time he yields with his hands and allows the pony to walk forward. As soon as the pony obeys, the rider's legs should cease squeezing and just maintain a light contact with his pony's sides.

Above left Bending down to touch the toe – another very good suppling exercise. It is very important to maintain the correct leg position throughout the exercise.

Left A group of riders cantering happily up the side of a field. Always ask permission to ride on other people's land, or use 'defined' bridle paths (those marked on an official map).

The simplest of the downward transitions, that from a walk to a halt, is frequently badly executed. It is therefore worth spending time to get this transition done well before progressing to more difficult ones. We have said the rider should follow the movement of the pony's head with his hands. To decrease the pace this movement must be resisted, but not by pulling on the reins. The first action must be to sit in a resisting position. The spine is straightened, which pushes the hips towards the hands. The hands then decrease their movement and thus resist the movement of the pony's head. The legs must also be ready to act, to ensure that the pony does not swing his quarters to one side; just gently close your legs on his sides to keep him up to the bit and straight. The pony should decrease pace when he feels the resistance from the hands, and should halt straight and square. As soon as he has obeyed, relax the pressure with your legs and reins.

The combination of the aids described are used for all increases and decreases of pace, with a slight variation for the canter when a particular leg is required.

The aids and school movements Harmony of the aids is also required when changing direction. The pony must always look in the direction in which he is going. To turn to the left the rider's left hand is carried outwards, leading the pony's nose to the left, and the pony should follow it in a gentle turn. This is called the *open rein*; as a rider progresses he learns to produce the same effect without moving his hand out. The rider's hands must work in harmony: if, as in this case, the left hand asks for a bend, then the right hand must allow the bend, by yielding a little without losing contact. At the same time the legs must maintain the forward movement, and ensure that the pony's hindfeet follow in the track of the forefeet. The rider's outside leg, the right leg in this case, is drawn a little behind the girth to prevent the hindquarters swinging out, while the inside leg, the left one, is kept on the girth to maintain forward movement.

This aid, known as the *diagonal aid*, when each hand and leg have a different function to perform but all are performed in harmony with each other, is used throughout equitation.

Care must be taken to ensure that aids are not used in opposition to each other. When asking for a bend with one rein, the other rein must allow that bend; similarly with the legs, if one leg asks for a lateral movement, then the other leg must allow it.

The study and practice of the aids is essential if they are to be applied with tact. Always remember that the seat and legs initiate a movement, the hands, through the reins, guide and control it.

Only by learning to ride on a reasonably well-trained pony can a novice rider learn to feel the effects of applying the aids. It is impossible to expect untrained riders to ride green ponies. Only an experienced horse will respond properly to aids given by a learner, which may be jerky and uneven.

The paces

The walk The rider should learn to sit correctly, and be able to turn and circle at the walk before attempting to trot. The walk is an easy pace with a four-time beat; that is, each foot is put down independently, and at no time are all four feet off the ground together.

The rider must sit upright with the weight squarely on both seat bones; with the head held up and the eyes looking straight ahead. The natural tendency is to lean forward, but this will weaken the seat and put more weight on the pony's forehand. It will also put the rider out of balance and make it impossible to apply the correct aids.

Riding like this at the walk will soon develop balance and confidence, and practising the exercises given on page 48 will help to accustom the rider to the feel of the saddle. Lengthening the reins by allowing them to slide through the fingers, then quietly taking them up again to the correct length will help to develop an independence of the hands.

The Trot: *learning to trot* When the beginner can proficiently perform the exercises and movements discussed at the walk with confidence, then some trot work may be attempted. The trot is a two-time pace, the legs moving in diagonal pairs, with a period of suspension when there are no feet on the ground. A balancing exercise, of rising in the stirrups at the halt, the rider at first holding on to the mane, should be practised until the rider can do it without holding on to the mane.

The ideal is then for the rider to be put on an experienced lunge pony to get the *feel* of the trot. It is a help if the stirrups are tied to the girth with a bit of string for the first few times. This will help prevent too much movement of the lower leg. The rider should sit upright in the saddle and hold the reins in one hand, and with the other hand, hook two fingers under the pommel of the saddle. To begin with, it is best for the rider to get the *feel* with a sitting trot, which means that he sits down in the saddle, not rising. He should hold himself down into the saddle, keeping the body upright and the eyes looking forward.

With the pony walking quietly round, the rider can use the same aids as he used when he asked for the pony to walk forward; squeeze with the calf muscles and at the same time yield with the reins.

The pony should trot forward; after a few strides the pony should be asked to walk again by applying the same aids as for the downward transition to the halt. This exercise can be repeated with the time of trotting increased until the rider feels quite confident to trot round a few circles. Once he has the feel of the sitting trot it is easier for the novice rider to do a rising trot.

Rising trot In the rising trot the body is inclined slightly forward and the rider lets himself be pushed up on one beat, then sits again for the next beat. As in the balancing exercise above, it is best to hold the reins in one hand, and the mane in the other.

When the pony is walking quietly, apply the aids to increase the pace, then, when the pony is trotting, begin rising. It will take a little while for the rider to establish the rhythm, but when he has, he can take a rein in either hand, and let go of the mane. It is very important to see at this stage that the rider only maintains a light contact with the pony's mouth, and does not pull himself up on the reins.

Keeping in balance during the rising trot is not easy. The lower leg position must be maintained against the sides of the pony, with the weight of the body lowering the heel. The forward and upward movement must come from the hips, not by pinching with the knee and bending the body forward. The rider must keep his head up and eyes looking forward; if he drops his head his shoulders will become round, and he will lose the influence of his seat. At this stage the sitting trot should only be used during increases and decreases of pace.

When the rider has established the rhythm of the trot, he can practise the exercises (page 48) he has done at the walk and halt. He should practise both turns and circles, riding to the markers, then making turns which are definite but smooth.

Turns and circles at trot When circling or turning, the rider should sit squarely, not inclining to the inside by collapsing the inside hip, as some beginners tend to

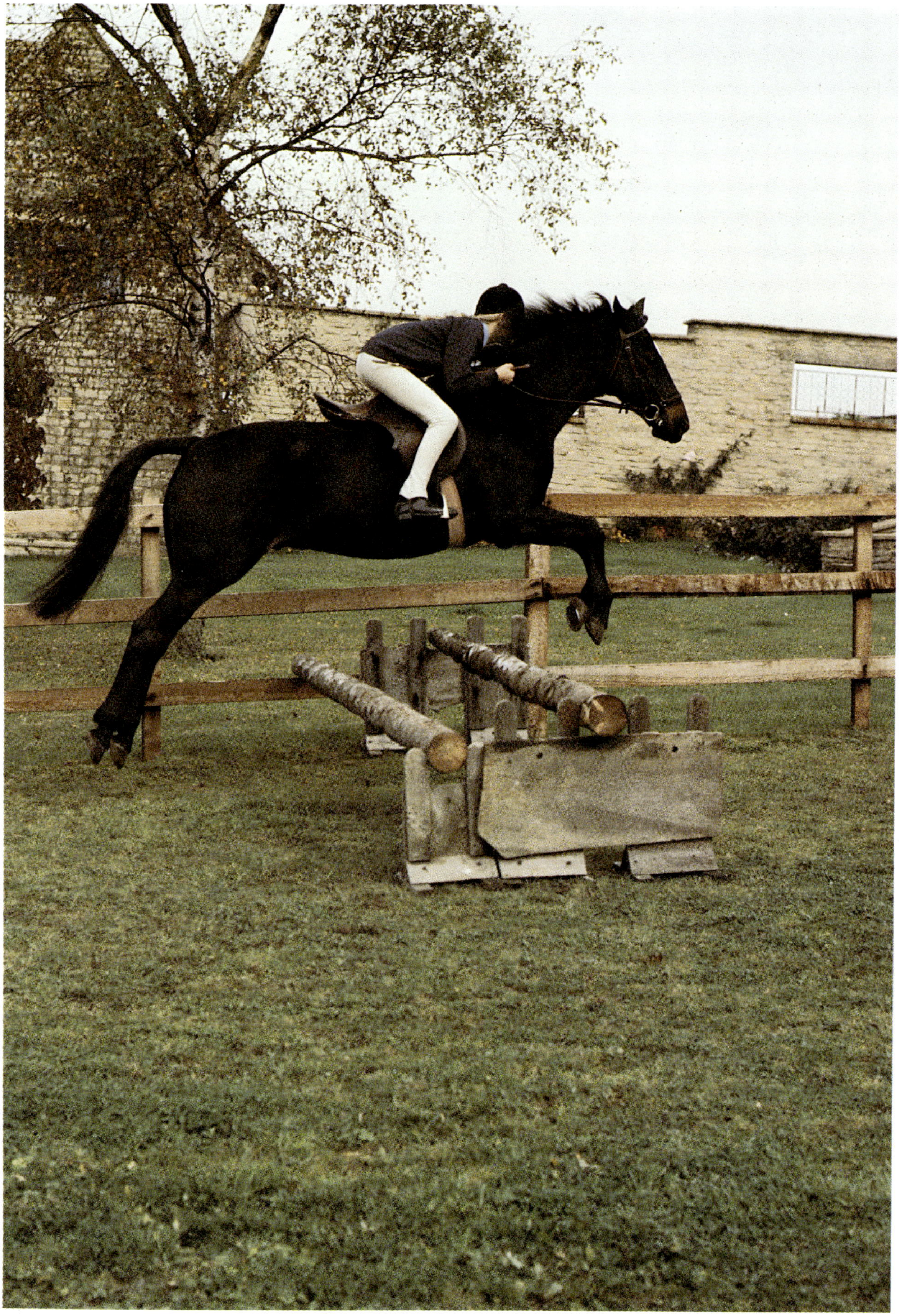

Above A good example of a pony using trotting poles correctly. In this case it is made easier by using post-and-rails fencing along one side and poles on the ground as a guide on the other side.

Left A sensible low fence for learning to jump. Note that the rider's hands are following the movement of the pony's head.

do. He should look in the direction in which he is going. The inside rein guides the pony in the direction in which he is going, the outside rein maintaining contact but allowing the bend. The inside leg remains on the girth to prevent the pony falling in on the circle, while the outside leg maintains impulsion and prevents the hindquarters from swinging out.

Turns, circles and changes of direction should all be executed accurately but smoothly, the pony bent in the direction in which it is going; but the curve of the pony's neck should never be greater than that of the rest of its spine.

Trot transitions Also practise making increases and decreases of pace. When both legs are applied and the hands eased, the horse should trot forward. A schooling whip may be used to reinforce the aid if the pony does not respond immediately. When the correct pace is achieved the rider can start rising, the legs ready to maintain the correct pace.

To decrease the pace to a walk the rider should cease rising, straighten his back and close his legs slightly to keep the pony straight. At the same time he resists with his hands until the pony walks, then yields with the hands and follows the movement of the pony's head in the new pace. These two transitions are very important to all work and must be practised with tact until they are perfected.

Trotting poles Riding over trotting poles is a very valuable exercise for both pony and rider. Begin with one pole, then gradually build them up to six. The rider's natural inclination is to lean back and pull on the reins, but this must not be permitted; instead, the rider must be taught to incline the body forward and yield with the reins. The poles should be spaced 4ft–5ft 6in (120–170cm) apart depending on the length of stride of the pony. Begin by walking over one pole, then trotting over it, the rider should get the feel of the pony stretching out over the pole. Particular attention must be paid to the rider's position; when he is in balance with the pony, then the poles can be increased in number. Trotting poles are of enormous help when a young pony is being taught to jump, to teach him to take them calmly and smoothly.

The canter Most riders find the canter an exciting pace, and frequently attempt it before they have established a firm seat at the trot.

The canter has a rocking motion. It is a three-time pace, and a pony can lead with either front leg; to enable him to turn quickly and safely he should canter with the inside front leg. There is a slight increase of pace from the trot, and the pony swings his head. The rider must allow the swing of the head and must learn to move in harmony with the rocking motion, whilst sitting upright with soft knees and hips.

The best place to begin a canter is on a circle or coming out of a bend so the pony is correctly positioned to lead on the inside leg. The rider is best to take both reins in the inside hand and hold himself into the saddle with the outside hand. From a sitting trot apply both legs, the inside one on the girth and the outside one behind the girth. As the pony goes forward, yield with the reins and pull the pelvis forward with the hand on the saddle.

In the canter the rider's back and loins must be supple to accommodate the rocking motion. The back must remain stretched upright with the head held high. The head and shoulders should appear to be still, the swing coming from the waist. Rounding or swinging of the shoulders will cause stiffness and will prevent the rider from giving the correct aids.

Many riders are inclined, wrongly, to hang on to the pony's head when cantering and not to follow the movement with the hands, which they should. This will cause the pony to lean on the rider, who in turn will increasingly hang on to the reins, thus setting up a vicious circle of incorrect riding and movement of the pony.

Canter transitions The same principles are followed for the downward transition to the trot as in the other downward transitions. However, from the canter, the use of the spine will be more effective, the rider straightening the spine and sitting deeply into the saddle, the seat pushed to the front. The legs close lightly on the pony's sides to keep him straight, the hands resist the movement of the head, and the pony decreases pace in a balanced manner with his hocks underneath him.

Cantering should only be practised for very short periods to begin with. Practising the transitions to and from the trot will help the rider to gain his balance and adjust to the change of rhythms.

Length of stirrups As a rider develops his seat and his muscles adjust to riding, he will be able to lengthen his stirrups by a few holes for the flat work, that is, riding on the ground as opposed to jumping. Care must be taken not to do this too soon, or by too much at once, as this will cause the rider to tip forward and will weaken his seat.

Equally, when a rider is to jump or ride cross-country he should shorten his stirrups so that he can carry the weight further forward, freeing the pony's loins and hindquarters to propel the pony forward. If the stirrups are shortened too much or too soon the rider will be pushed to the back of the saddle, causing him to be insecure. The established rider can therefore lengthen his stirrups for school work and shorten them for jumping or hunting.

Jumping

First steps If the work over trotting poles has been thoroughly established, then it is only a small step to progress to jumping. A pole about 15in (40cm) high should be placed 6 feet (2m) from the last trotting pole. The rider quietly trots over the poles, then over the jump.

Over the trotting poles the rider learnt to incline his body forwards with a little more weight on the knee and thigh down into the stirrup, the heel thus sinking a little and tightening the calf muscles. As the pony takes off over the jump the angle between the rider's body and his thigh closes, the hands follow the movement of the pony's head forward, but there is a minimum of movement from the rider's body itself. There should be no sudden thumping of the rider's legs as the pony comes into a fence. He should maintain a light contact, and as the jumps get bigger, he should use his legs in rhythm with the pony's stride.

Once the rider has the feel of trotting over poles and a small fence, then the fence can be enlarged a little. A parallel about 20in (50cm) high and wide will make the pony round himself over the fence more, and so give the rider the feel of a little more movement with the pony's head and neck.

Great care must be taken to see that the rider rides accurately on the flat both before and after the jump, that he turns correctly and approaches the fence straight, then continues straight after the fence.

When the rider has learnt to cope with one small fence, then another may be introduced one canter stride away, about 22ft (6.5m). As he progresses, the fences may be changed and enlarged a little, and the number of strides in between them varied. Eventually the rider should learn to count the strides in between fences, and the number of squeezes he gives the pony with his lower leg. The rider's seat must return to the saddle between fences, and the hands follow the movement of the head and neck at all times. If something goes wrong and the rider gets out of balance then he must learn to slip the reins through his fingers so as not to hurt his pony's mouth.

When the rider can efficiently jump several fences up to 3ft (1m) in height, then he should be developing an eye for distance and begin to judge his stride.

Jumping a simple course The next step is to teach the rider to take the pony round a simple course. The fences should be kept small but have spreads (i.e., be wide) and the rider should bring the pony back to a trot after every fence, allowing him to canter the last two strides into each fence. Up until now the trotting poles have kept the pony calm and straight before a fence; now it will be up to the rider. The most important part of jumping a fence is the approach; this must be calm and obedient. The rider should bring the pony to the fence in balance and at the right speed, with sufficient impulsion to clear the fence. The rider must keep his seat firmly in the saddle, the lower leg urging the pony forward in rhythm with the stride, his hands and elbows soft, ready to follow the movement of the head.

As the rider gains experience he will learn to see his stride, to judge whether he

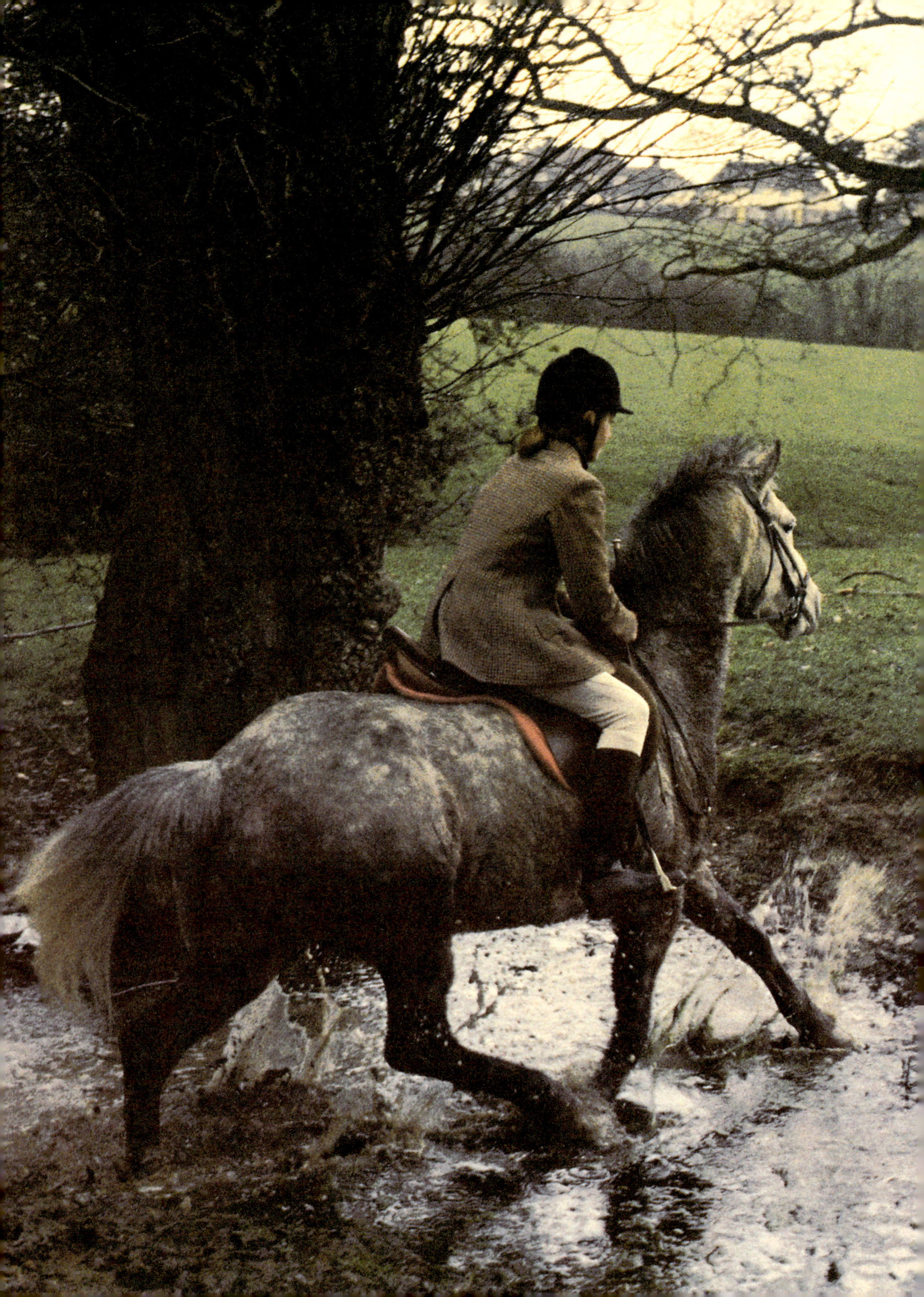

This shallow stream is an ideal place to introduce a pony to going through water. The first few times this is attempted it is a great help for a friend on an experienced horse to give him a lead; ponies will often follow another where they are frightened to go on their own.

is going to meet the fence correctly or not. In time he will learn to lengthen or shorten the stride of the pony to meet the fence correctly.

Only when both pony and rider are quite confident jumping small fences in the school, should solid cross-country fences be attempted. Most ponies are more keen outside, especially when in company. The rider must keep his mount between hand and leg, to begin with at the trot, then at a canter, gradually building up towards going at a gallop.

The gallop is achieved by increasing the speed of the canter until each foot comes to the ground separately in a four-time rhythm. There is a period of suspension when all four feet are off the ground. The pony should lead with the inside foreleg, as in the canter.

The rider must remain in balance, although his body is inclined forward with the seat bones just raised out of the saddle to allow complete freedom of the pony's back and loins. The heel must remain lower than the toe, with the ankle and knee acting as shock absorbers. A fault frequently seen is the rider with too long a stirrup leather, standing in his stirrups with the toe pointing downwards.

When a rider has had some experience of riding cross-country and has a good relationship with his pony, he can start entering for small competitions or hunter trials, provided he gets his pony fit. See pages 97 and 108.

5
PONY CARE AND EQUIPMENT

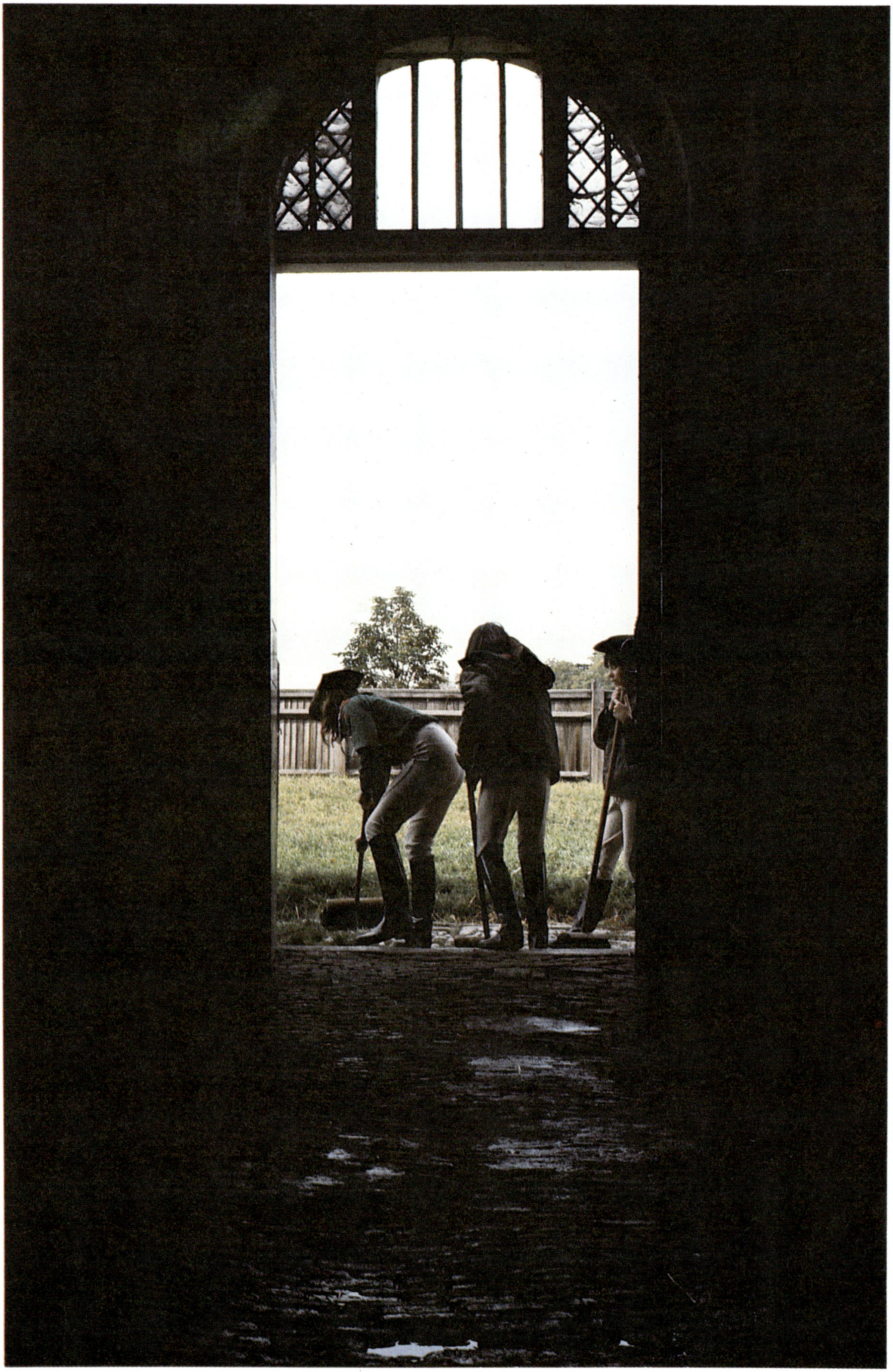

PONY CARE AND EQUIPMENT

Anyone lucky enough to have their own pony has a responsibility to that animal, to look after it properly. Most children at some stage of their lives own, or have an interest in a pet. It may be a mouse or hamster, or a family dog; all these animals live in the house, and can be attended to quite easily with no great effort.

A pony is very different; it does not fall into the category of a pet, and nobody should be under the illusion that it can be treated like any other pet. A dog is said to be man's best friend; a dog can spend nearly all day, and in some cases, the night, in close proximity to its master; unless one can spend all day every day with a pony, this cannot be the case with our equine friends.

KEEPING A PONY AT GRASS

Suitable grazing

A suitable and proper place to keep a pony is the first essential to arrange before contemplating acquiring one. If you are lucky enough to live on a farm or have your own paddocks, then this problem is easily overcome. For those less fortunate there are a number of alternatives; ponies like to have company, so you may be able to make arrangements with someone who already has horses, to keep your pony with theirs. A local farmer may allow you to graze your pony on his land, or you may be able to buy or rent a paddock yourself. If the latter is the case, then you should bear a number of factors in mind. The first is that you must visit your pony at least once a day in the summer, and twice a day in the winter, so you should be able to do this conveniently. The paddock should be of a suitable size, two to three acres (about one hectare) per pony if possible; if it is less then you will have to feed him more. The herbage should be in good condition; if ponies have been kept there for a number of years, then the ground should have a change of animal grazing it, or be ploughed up and re-seeded.

It is best to have more than one field to keep ponies in so that each field can be rested. Ponies are wasteful feeders and trample a lot more grass than they need in their search for the best tasting grass. If only one field is available, then it is best if it can be divided into three; one part to be grazed whilst the other two are being rested. Hay can probably be made off one section when there is more than enough grass in the summer.

If it is a small area then it is advisable to pick up the droppings as they will foul up the grazing, but this is not practical for large areas, where the field should be harrowed occasionally.

It will need an expert to advise on the quality of the grazing. If the pasture should need re-seeding, then it is best to use one of the mixtures of grass seed especially prepared for horse grazing.

Fencing and shelter

The fences should be in good repair. A good thick hedge will not only prevent a pony straying, but will also provide shelter from the winds and rain in the winter,

All stabling, whether modern or old, needs to be kept scrupulously clean, for safety and hygiene reasons. These Horse Rangers are cleaning the Royal Mews stables of their headquarters at Hampton Court, which date from the sixteenth century, and have old-fashioned stalls; loose boxes are the kind of stabling generally preferred nowadays.

and shade in the summer. Post and rails are the best alternative, but they are expensive, and some form of shelter will be necessary as well. Less expensive are posts with plain wire, which must be strained tightly; the bottom wire should be not less than a foot (30cm) off the ground to prevent the pony getting caught up in it. Barbed-wire and chicken or pig wire are not suitable and should be avoided.

A good thick hedge or belt of trees are usually preferred by ponies to a shed for shelter, but in the absence of such natural shelter, then some form must be provided. An open shed, with its back to the prevailing wind is normally the most practical, and will be in much demand by ponies in summer to keep out of the sun and away from the flies.

Dangerous plants and rubbish

Your paddock must also be free from poisonous plants and any foreign bodies. Most hedgerows have their share of poisonous plants or trees; the most common of these, and also most deadly is the yew tree; but rhododendron, laburnum, ivy, deadly nightshade, hemlock, bryony and ragwort can all prove fatal. Check your field very thoroughly for signs of these and get them thoroughly removed before you put your pony in the field; if there is ragwort, it will need to be pulled regularly during the summer. This has small yellow flowers and grows about two feet (60cm) tall. It is all too often too late when you notice your pony is not well and call in the vet.

All the rubbish left by people is also a very common source of injury to ponies in fields. The broken bottles, plastic bags, discarded tins and other sharp objects left behind by picnickers or carelessly thrown over the hedge, account for numerous injuries to ponies. You should walk round your paddock every day to check that everything is alright, that the fences are all intact and that there are no dangerous foreign bodies lying around.

Drinking water

Also essential in your field is a good, constant supply of clean water. Although your pony may not drink very much in the winter and when the grass is wet, he will drink upwards of ten gallons (45.5 litres) a day in the summer, and to rely on a bucket of water filled once or twice a day is not enough. A proper water trough with piped water is the best; the trough must be cleaned out regularly and kept free of leaves and slime. A running stream or brook, provided the water is not contaminated by drains or other effluent, is also acceptable but stagnant ponds are not suitable.

Day-to-day care

Having arranged a suitable paddock in which to keep your pony, you must next concern yourself with the day-to-day care that he will need.

Most mountain and moorland ponies (that is, native British breeds) will be able to live out of doors all the year round under normal weather conditions. In their wild state they have to be hardy to survive; during the summers they grow fat and sleek on the unlimited summer grass, but during the winter they lose condition and only the fittest will live to the next year. This has ensured that only the strongest have gone on to reproduce another generation.

However, if we have a pony to ride then we expect him to carry not only himself, but also a rider; to do this he must be kept in good condition all the year round. If he is only ridden at weekends, for quiet hacking, a good grass pasture should provide him with all he needs in the summer. During the winter he will need supplementary feeding, according to the condition of the pasture, the climate and the type and amount of work asked of him.

A pony with half or more of Thoroughbred or Arab blood will not be happy to be left in a field all the year. During the winter he will need to be stabled at night, and may well need a New Zealand rug on him when he is turned out in the daytime. This we will discuss later, see pages 71 and 72.

As the summer is the time of year when children ride most frequently, we will deal with that first.

Extra feeding in summer

If your pony is going to be ridden every day, and probably go to a show or gymkhana at the weekends, then he will need some extra hard food in the summer. Grass is soft food, and is inclined to make a pony fat. If he will have to carry you and perform for you, then, to give him the extra energy, you will have to give him extra food.

The traditional foods for horses for many years have been oats, beans and peas. All these have the effect of making them excitable and of *hotting* them up. Whereas this may be alright for a racehorse who has to produce great speed to win on a race-course, or for a hunter expected to cover anything up to fifty miles (80km) in a day, it is not advisable for a pony at grass.

Every pony is different, and what will be enough for one will be too much or not enough for another. You can always give your pony a little more, so begin with a little and build it up till you feel that he has enough stamina without being silly.

One of the easiest forms of feeding your pony is with cubes, as these give a balanced diet. Be careful to see that you buy the correct type of cube for your pony; if you give him some designed for racehorses or for stud purposes, then they will not give him the proper nutrients that he needs. A very rough guide for a pony at grass who is working every day would be to give him 2–4lbs (1–2kg) of cubes with $\frac{1}{2}$lb (200g) of damped bran, and some sliced apples or carrots.

Barley is another good food for ponies, as it is not as heating as oats; it must never be fed whole, as it can cause serious colic. Barley may be fed either rolled or crushed by the millers, or it may be boiled until the kernel splits open, in which case it must be cooled sufficiently before it is fed so the pony does not burn himself.

When the grass is growing well and there is plenty, your pony will probably reject a net of hay. Provided there is a good selection of herbage, with a great variety of leafy grasses mixed with some clovers, this will provide him with all the bulk he needs, and rich sweet grass is always preferable to hay.

As we have said, during the summer your pony will not be likely to need any hay, unless you stable him overnight before a show or some other function. However it is wise to organize the supply of hay you will be needing during the winter months, whilst hay is plentiful in the summer. A local farmer is probably the best person to approach; if he is not able to supply you himself, then he can probably put you in touch with someone who can. Storing hay properly is most important; however good the hay may be, unless it is correctly stored it will be of little use to you or your pony. Unless you have somewhere to store it, it is best to leave it in the rick and collect a few bales as you need them. You will need to work out how much your pony will eat, an average 12–13 hands pony will probably need about 10lbs (4.5kg) a day; more in bad weather, and he will need feeding from November till the grass comes again in May. So if you reckon on buying a ton (1 tonne) of hay, that should be enough to see him through the winter. See also page 71.

Feeding in winter

During the winter months, grass does not grow, and there will be little or no food value in what there is. Your pony will need to be fed hay twice a day; the best

Left These ponies are standing in a trailer between classes at a show. They are wearing summer sheets to keep their coats smooth and protect them from the flies.

Below Riders leading their ponies out from the stable ready to mount up. Note that the stirrups are correctly run-up so they cannot catch on any doorways or gateposts. The two loose boxes are solidly built and have a small yard with a stout fence, useful for tying-up ponies while mucking-out or grooming in summer. The building and yard are well-maintained and clean and tidy.

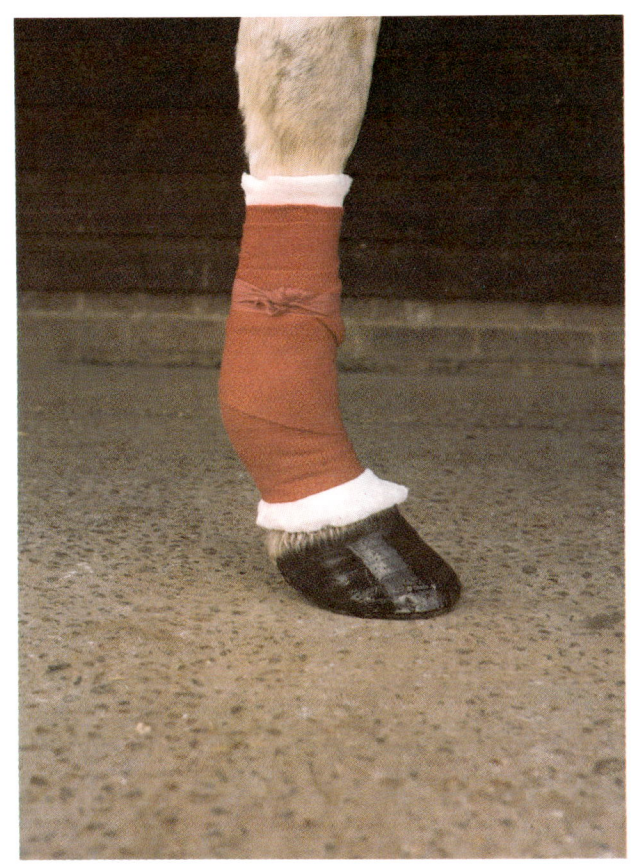

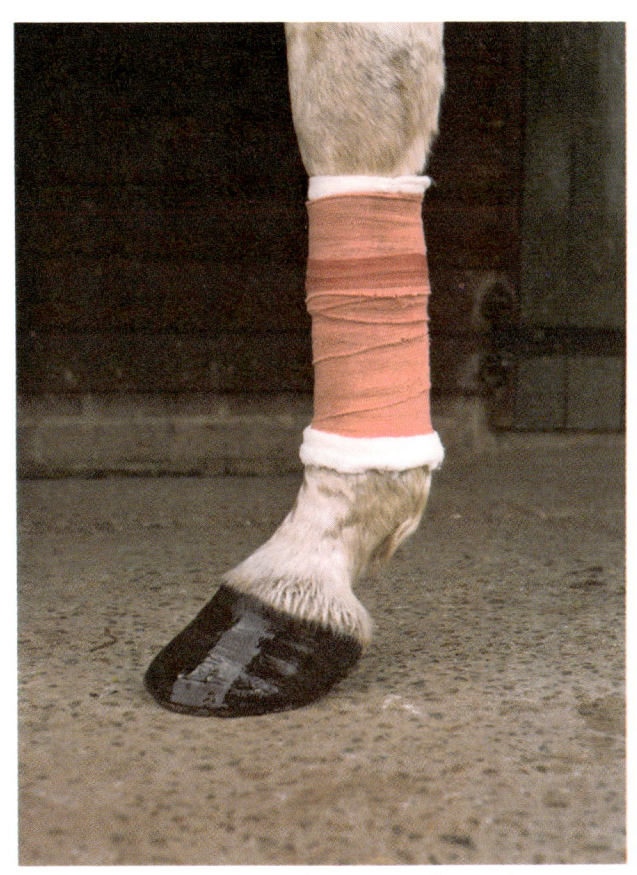

Above A stable bandage, used for travelling in a box or trailer, to dry off wet or muddy legs and for warmth in the stable for a pony with a cold. It should afford protection to the pastern. It is made of flannel and a layer of gamgee tissue or cotton wool goes underneath. The knot must be tied on the outside and the ends tucked in.

Above right An exercise bandage, which requires great experience to apply correctly. They support the tendons and protect the legs between the knee or hock, and the fetlock. They are made of stockinette or crepe and have a layer of gamgee tissue or cotton wool underneath.

method is to put it in a haynet which should be tied up securely so there is no chance of your pony getting his foot caught in it if he should paw the ground. A small net of hay given in the morning, together with a small feed of concentrates, should keep him happy during the daytime. The bulk of the hay, together with a larger feed of concentrates, is best fed in the evening.

Much of the food fed to your pony will be used to keep him warm, so the colder and more unpleasant the weather the more food he will need. Again, the quantity of concentrates he needs will depend on many factors; the amount of grazing, the quality of the hay, the type of pony and the amount of work you expect him to do. Sugar-beet pulp or nuts are an excellent form of food during the winter; these must be very thoroughly soaked for twenty-four hours before they are fed. If they are not properly soaked, they swell inside the pony's stomach, and can burst the stomach; in any event your pony may suffer a very painful death.

A warm feed of boiled barley mixed with bran or a linseed bran mash, will be most acceptable to your pony during very cold weather. Minerals are also most essential during the winter, and either a salt and mineral lick or a block of *Keep* will help your pony to put the food you give him to the best use.

Summer ailments

You may think that with a suitable field, plenty to eat and drink then you have provided everything your pony needs, but it is essential to look at your pony at least once a day in summer, twice in winter and see that he has not damaged himself and has no cuts or swellings. In hot weather, flies cause great misery to ponies, and an application of fly repellent can do much to alleviate this nuisance. Make sure that everything in the field is alright, all the gates properly shut, no broken bottles or tins and that the water tank is clean and full.

Care must be taken in summer to see that your pony does not get too fat. Most mountain and moorland ponies have grown accustomed to living on poor pasture, where they have adapted themselves to make the most out of the food available. On good rich pasture they are inclined to over-eat and become overweight; this causes unnecessary strain on their limbs, heart and internal organs. If your pony is beginning to get too fat, then you must cut down his hours of grazing. During the hot summer months, one of the best systems of doing this is to bring him into a stable during the day, when the flies are bad, just providing him with plenty of fresh water, then allow him out to graze again in the evening.

A common but painful complaint that many overweight ponies suffer from is an inflammation of the sensitive part of the foot, known as laminitis. The foot is contained within the hard wall of the hoof, and as this cannot expand, great discomfort is caused, and permanent damage to the foot may result. The pony should be removed from the field, and all access to food denied. He should have plenty of water to drink, then, after a day without food, small bran mashes should be given twice a day. Standing him in a stream, or running cold water over his feet will help to reduce the inflammation and ease the pain. Gradual introduction of walking exercise will help to get his body functioning properly once again.

Grass-kept ponies are also inclined to get skin complaints during the summer. Humour is a pimply condition of the skin, normally due to over-eating or grass that is too rich. It is best treated by adding some Epsom or Glauber salts to the pony's water. About 2–4oz (60–120gm) given daily will usually clear up this condition.

Itchy manes and tails can also be caused by over-heating of the blood due to too much food. A thorough wash with a medicated shampoo may help, combined with keeping the area free of scurf and dirt. Lice are usually found only on ponies in poor condition, but they can easily be spread from one pony to another, so always be on the look-out for them; an application of a good anti-parasite powder should deal with them.

Sweet-itch is a distressing complaint and one for which there is as yet no definite cure. It is a severe irritation in the area of the neck, mane, withers and dock, and is frequently accompanied by a yellow discharge. The affected animals rub these areas raw; it would appear to be aggravated by certain small flies. The only treatment available at the moment is to keep the pony out of the sun and the flies during the daytime and in the early evening. The vet will be able to give you some medicaments to apply to the affected area to alleviate the irritation.

The winter coat and clipping

During the autumn your pony will begin to grow his thick winter coat. This, along with the natural grease that forms on his skin, will help to protect him from the winter elements. Grooming in late autumn and winter is best kept to a minimum, just removing the surface mud on his coat, picking out his feet and keeping his mane and tail free of tangles.

The heavy winter coat that your pony will have grown for protection will obviously limit the amount of work that he can undertake. Strenuous work will cause undue sweating and result in a loss of condition, so ponies who are expected to do fast work regularly will need to be partially clipped, and consequently have to be stabled at night. A 'trace clip' is usual, in which hair is removed from under the belly, the gullet and under the chin.

However, there is no reason why you should not take your unclipped pony for the odd day's hunting, provided you feed him correctly and have him reasonably fit. The thing to remember is not to stay out till the end of the day, returning home in the dark. Come home reasonably early, give him a chilled drink (water which has been warmed to take the chill off) then clean the worst of the mud off and check for any cuts or thorns, give him a bran mash, then turn him out. He will probably go and roll in the dirtiest place he can find, but so long as he has his haynet and his usual feed later, he should come to little harm.

Ponies that are hunted regularly will need to be clipped and stabled at night. They can then be turned out in the daytime in a New Zealand rug, to exercise themselves. This method works very satisfactorily, but obviously necessitates more work. The pony will need to be rugged at night, have his rugs changed night and morning and be mucked out every day. All these items will be dealt with in more detail later in this chapter.

KEEPING A STABLED PONY

Those ponies who are expected to do quite a lot of work in the winter, and those that are not suited to living out all the year round will need to be stabled at night time.

Ponies in their natural state have roamed free for thousands of years; if we are to deny them that freedom by keeping them in a stable, then we must look after them in a manner that compensates for that loss of freedom. A pony shut up in a stable for twenty-three hours each day will get very bored. Ponies are happier if they can be turned out in a paddock for the day and be brought into a stable at night. Horses or ponies that are stabled all the time must be professionally looked after, and be kept with other horses.

Not everyone is able to erect their *ideal* stable, but some basic requirements are essential. The stable must be big enough, not less than 12 × 10ft (3.6 × 3m); and must be high enough so the pony does not bump his head if he throws it up. The door must be wide enough for him to walk through without any chance of banging his hips; the correct width of a stable door is 4ft (1.2m).

Do make sure the roof is sound and will not leak, or terrify him by blowing away in a gale. Also try to check that there can be no draughts, such as two doors opposite each other; if there are, then seal one of them up. Look carefully round the stable for sharp or protruding objects that he might injure himself on. You will need a manger for his feed, but a heavy old sink can serve for this. You will also need somewhere high up for tying his haynet, and a ring where you tie him to groom him.

Bedding

A stabled pony will also need bedding. The most usual is wheat straw, barley straw can cause skin irritations and your pony will probably eat oat straw. If straw is not available or is not suitable then wood shavings, sawdust or peat may be used. Whatever is used, there must be plenty to give a good deep bed, and it should be banked well up the sides to help prevent the pony becoming *cast*.

Stable routine

It is important to develop a routine for your pony when he is stabled. As you will probably be at school for much of the time, then it is only sensible to make it as simple as possible. Before your breakfast, say between 7.00am and 7.30am go to the stable and check that your pony is alright. You can then feed him; it is probably best to tie him up while he is feeding, then you sill be able to do the mucking out. When he has finished his food and you have swept up and put the stable tidy, then he can be turned out in his field, which is essential for exercise when he is not ridden during the day. If he is clipped or it is very cold then he should have a New Zealand rug.

When you return from school is the best time to get your pony in from the field, before he gets too cold. It is easiest to get the stable completely ready for him while

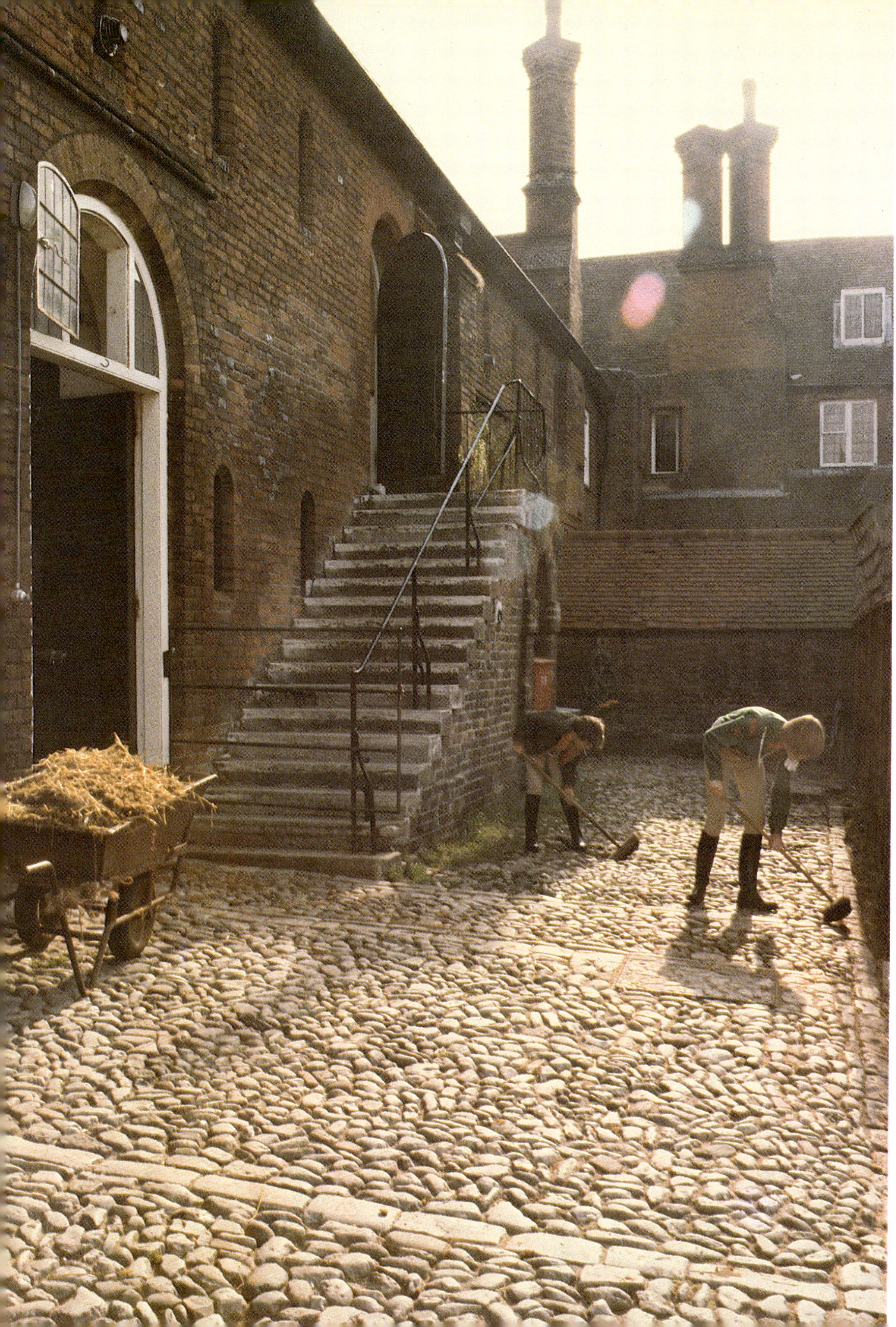

Left Horse Rangers hard at work sweeping the old cobbled stable yard of their headquarters at Hampton Court. This is the only uniformed horse youth movement in the world. It is a registered charity supported by a variety of fund-raising events, in many of which members take part.

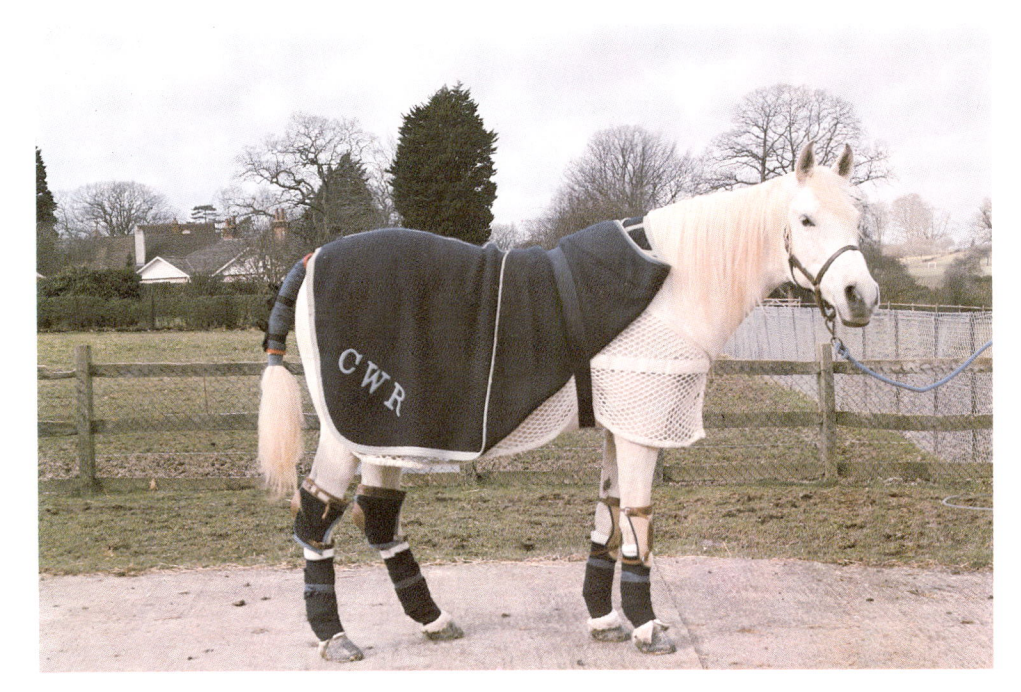

Above right A pony prepared to travel, with an anti-sweat rug underneath the day rug. The front of the day rug has been turned back to prevent him sweating around his shoulders. He is wearing a tail bandage, made of crepe, and hock boots and knee caps as well as stable bandages.

Right A New Zealand rug, made of waterproof canvas lined with wool. Waterproof quilted nylon ones are also available. The rug must fit well over the withers to prevent the chest being rubbed. The fillet straps (round the hind legs) prevent the rug blowing up in a wind.

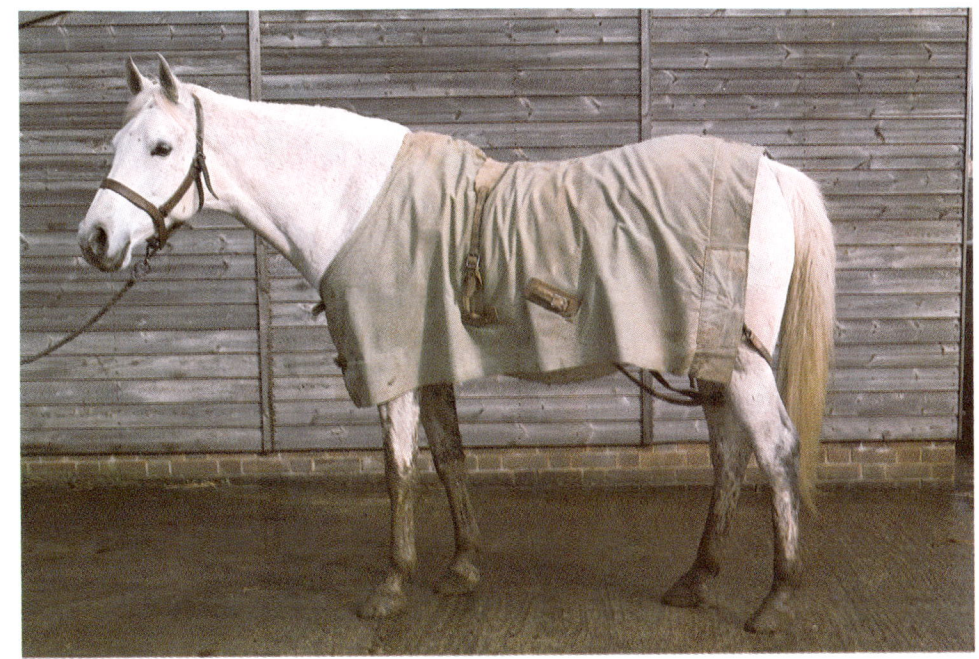

it is empty. Do this in the morning if you have time. First put down more bedding, then fill the water bucket and haynet. Now you can fetch your pony from the field, check him over, pick out his feet and give him a brush over to put him tidy. If he has rugs these must be changed.

If the stable is close to hand then it is better to look at him and feed him later. This is probably best done at about 6.00–6.30pm. Take out any droppings, fill up the water buckets and give your pony his feed.

Feeding a stabled pony

The subject of feeding is a long and controversial one. In this book only the very basic requirements will be discussed.

The main food your pony will need is hay. There are many types that vary according to the different grasses in the hay. Quite a hard type of hay that contains rye grass, timothy and some clover is best. Soft or meadow hay is made from old pasture and is excellent for youngstock. The most important thing about any hay is that it should smell sweet. If it was baled damp then mildew will grow and the hay will smell fusty. Hay is one thing that should not be stinted on, buy the best you can and be sure to store it well. Your pony will need from 10–15lb (4.5–6.7kg) per day depending on his size.

The hard feed your pony will need will depend very much on how much work he gets. If he goes out in a field most days, then he will need about the same amount of food as a pony in a field. If he is worked every day, then he will need more. Feed according to his type, size and the work he does. See also page 65.

Stable rugs

If your pony is stabled at night then he will probably need some clothing. In the daytime a New Zealand rug will be most useful; it will not only keep him warm and dry, but will keep most of him clean. This is made of a heavy waterproof canvas, and lined with a wool blanket. It must fit snugly round the neck and should come over the front of the withers, so preventing the rug rubbing on the point of the shoulder. They may be fitted with a surcingle, attached along the backline, which should be done up loosely and is only there to prevent the rug blowing up in the wind. Thigh straps are attached to the back; these should be fitted between the hindlegs, looped through each other to prevent them rubbing, and attached to the D on the same side of the rug. These prevent the rug from blowing up or slipping.

If your pony is clipped he will also need rugs at night, although if he is only trace clipped he will only need them in very cold weather or after a day's hunting. A jute rug, lined with a wool material is the most usual; this will be kept in place with a roller, which may be made of leather or jute. Extra padding such as a folded sack, is also advisable, to put under the roller, on top of the rug, to protect the spine. If your pony has a full clip or you think he is cold, then he will need a thick wool blanket under his jute rug. This should be put on well forward and turned back over the jute rug before the roller is put on to help prevent it slipping too much.

There are also a number of insulated rugs on the market. These work on the same basis as a sleeping bag and are made of layers of lightweight material sandwiched between an outside and an inside layer. They usually have a surcingle attached; if it is the same material as the rug, it will be quite safe and not cause back damage. Should you buy one of these rugs, then do get one with a lining made of cotton; those with brushed nylon linings will cause the pony to sweat, because the skin cannot breathe through them.

COMMON AILMENTS

Mud fever and cracked heels

Two of the complaints that ponies may suffer from during the winter are mud fever and cracked heels. Mud fever is an irritation of the skin usually affecting the legs and sometimes the belly. It is more common in some areas than others, but is not an easy complaint to cure. Prevention is the best policy; covering the areas most likely to be affected with an oil or vaseline before going riding over wet ground should help to prevent this complaint as well as making it much easier to clean the pony afterwards. Cracked heels are caused by the tender skin in the heels of the pony becoming chapped and then cracked. An infection can then enter the wound and cause serious inflammation and lameness. Always be careful to dry your pony's heels thoroughly when you bring him into the stable. Both these complaints are more frequently found in ponies who are partially stabled, than in ponies who live out at grass all the time.

Worms

Another most important aspect, that must never be neglected, is that of worms. All horses and ponies carry worms to a varying degree. There are three main types, round worms, whip worms and red worms.

Round worms which are white in colour, they may be up to a foot (30cm) in length and the thickness of a pencil. In large numbers they can cause severe loss of condition and can cause a stoppage or bursting of the gut. The worm lays its eggs in the gut; these are then expelled in the droppings. They hatch in the pasture and the pony then re-infects himself by eating the larvae as he is grazing. The small worms enter the gut, penetrate the walls of the intestine and move through the internal organs until the process begins again.

Whip worms are only an inch or two (2.5–5cm) long and very thin. They live in the bowel of the horse. They do not do a lot of harm, but they cause irritation, making the horse rub its tail.

Red worms are the most dangerous of all. They are very small, only growing to half an inch (1.25cm) long. They feed by sucking blood, so giving them a red appearance. They follow the same life cycle as the round worms, but the larvae can cause great damage to the blood vessels of a horse, which can result in the rupture of a vein or artery, and subsequent death.

Bots

Another form of intestinal parasite is the stomach bot. This is the larvae of the gadfly, a quite large brownish-yellow fly, that lays its eggs on the skin of horses. These are small yellow specks, usually on the legs, that are quite hard to pick off. The eggs hatch out and the horse licks them off; thus they enter through the mouth. They burrow their way into the gums and tongue then later pass to the stomach, where in quantity they can cause considerable damage, even resulting in the rupture of the stomach.

All these intestinal parasites can be dealt with quite easily and effectively by the administration of worm preparations. These may be bought from your vet; adult ponies should be wormed ten to twelve times a year, slightly dependent on their condition and the state of the pasture. The control of worms is a most vital part of a pony's well being; the damage that is done by them is not visible from the outside, but it all too often proves fatal. Each time you buy a worm preparation get one containing different chemicals from the last to avoid immunity developing in the parasite.

Tetanus

Tetanus is another killer, and it is more prevalent in some areas than others. The tetanus bacillus live in the soil and enter the animal through a wound, usually a small puncture that closes up shortly after it has occurred and so goes unnoticed. Animals very rarely recover from this disease, and then are unlikely to return to their former well-being. A course of injections can immunize against this unpleasant disease, and all pony owners would be wise to ensure that their animals have been properly vaccinated. A booster dose should be given every other year.

Teeth

Your pony's teeth, unlike your own teeth, go on growing all his life. They can get worn unlevel and become sharp, thus rubbing the inside of his mouth and making it sore. You should get your vet to inspect your pony's teeth every year, and if it is necessary he will file off any sharp edges that may be causing your pony difficulty in eating his hay or hard feed.

Overleaf Riders returning from a ride in the Scottish Highlands, correctly running up their stirrups, and loosening the girths to let the ponies cool gradually. The two dapple greys are Highland ponies. These loose boxes have a widely overhanging roof to protect the open half-doors from the weather. The paved walkway is immaculately swept and orderly.

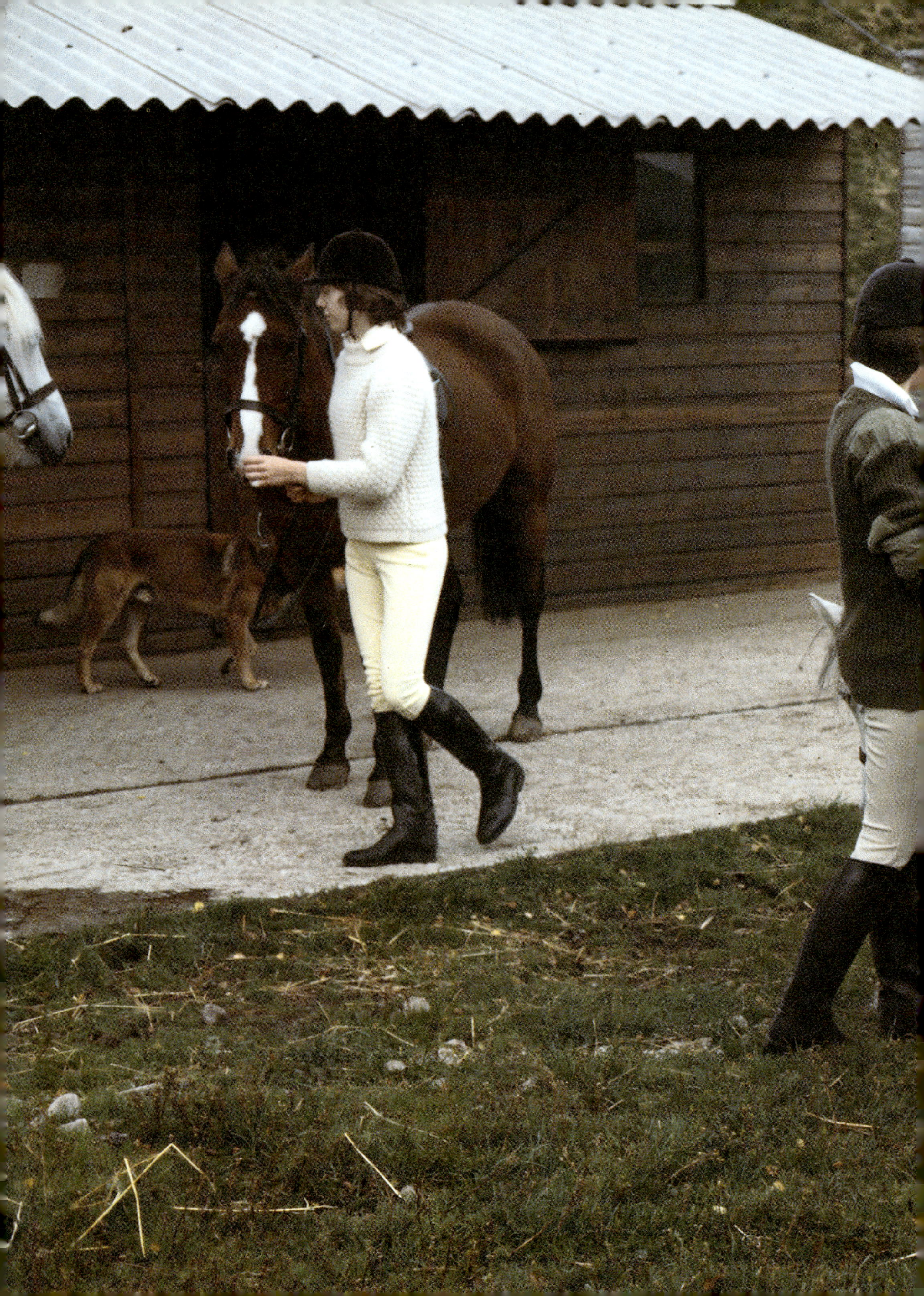

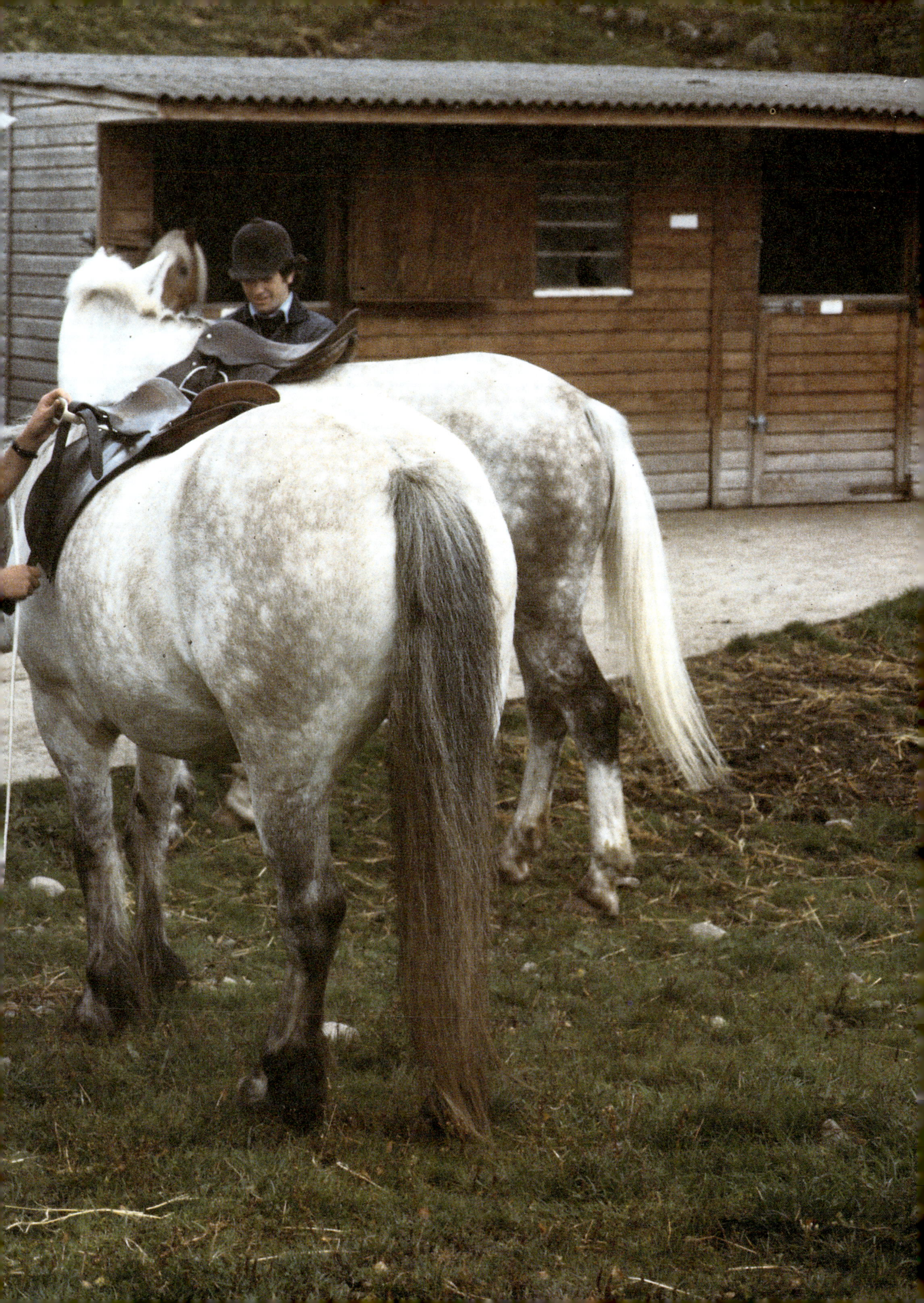

Feet

Last, but by no means least important, is the care of your pony's feet. That old adage *no foot, no horse* is as true today as when it was first said. Ponies who are only ridden on grass or other soft surfaces, and rarely go on the roads, will probably cope very well indeed without shoes. That does not mean to say that you can ignore their feet. The outside horn of the foot is constantly growing like our own nails. It can grow $\frac{1}{4}$in (6mm) each month, which will mean that it needs frequent care to keep it in shape. An unshod pony will wear his feet down a little with work, but more than likely, he will wear them unlevel; so attention from a farrier every six weeks is essential.

Most ponies are shod to protect their feet from the wear and tear they would receive by riding on roads. It is most important that this skilled task should be done by a good farrier. This may mean that you have to take your pony some way to a reputable farrier to get a good job done; but badly shod feet will only lead to trouble in the future.

Your pony's feet will keep growing, whether or not he has worn his shoes out. He will need his feet to be attended to every four to six weeks, depending on the amount of work, and how fast his feet grow. Every day when you look at your pony, you should check his feet to see that his shoes are alright. You are almost certain to have to book to go to the farrier, so it is no good leaving it until the day before you want to ride to discover that he has a shoe missing.

The ends of the nails that are turned over the horn are known as the *clenches*; these can *rise* and become a danger to your pony who may knock the opposite leg with them. If they are *risen* it is nearly always a sign that your pony needs a visit to the farrier to be re-shod.

General health care

In general, looking after a pony is a task that must be weighed up before you undertake it. The general rules laid down on paper will be a good guide to follow, but expert advice on occasions is invaluable. Beware of the pony owner who has learnt everything from the book; there is no substitute for years of thorough practical experience. Do make sure you can call upon the help of a vet or some knowledgeable person before you find yourself with a crisis on your hands; time wasted in finding help may be crucial. Get to know the signs of your particular pony's good health – a glossy coat, interest in surroundings, good appetite – so you learn to notice as soon as he is off-colour.

When your pony is out at grass, look carefully at the pony and his field every day. Whilst most ponies stay sound and healthy, there are occasions when they may be sick or lame. The average pony owner would not be expected to know what to do, but should be able to recognize when something is wrong, and then get expert advice.

If you see your pony standing in a corner or behind a hedge with his head down, looking miserable, then take a closer look at him. He may only be cold and wet, but he may have caught a chill or be suffering from some other ailment. If he is just cold and miserable, then he will perk up as you approach and will be happy to have his food. If however he doesn't seem interested in you or the food then there is probably something wrong so fetch some help.

Perhaps more difficult to recognize is if your pony is lame. If you are riding him and he goes lame, you should be able to feel that he is going with uneven steps and is putting more weight on one foot than the other. Get off him, look to see if he has got a stone wedged in his foot; if he has, remove it and he will probably go sound again. If this is not the cause of the trouble, then walk him slowly home or to the nearest farm and get some assistance.

If you see your pony standing with one front foot pointed forward in front of the other, then this is usually a sign of lameness, or you may notice when you are brushing him over that one leg is swollen; this is another sign of trouble, so do get expert help. The sooner that a lameness or illness can be treated, the better the chances of a quick recovery, so do always look to see if there seems to be anything unusual about your pony and take some action.

GROOMING

You will need to collect a grooming kit, to enable you to do the job correctly. The essentials are: a hoofpick, a dandy brush, a body brush, a metal curry comb, a mane comb and two sponges. Optional items are: a rubber curry comb, a water brush, a sweat scraper and a stable rubber.

When you groom your pony, first of all pick out his feet. Using a hoofpick, remove the mud and anything else wedged in his feet, working from the heel along the frog towards the toe. A length of coloured ribbon or string tied to the hoofpick will help to prevent you losing it too easily.

In winter a pony living out should have only very little grooming; see The winter coat and clipping, page 68.

During the summer your pony will have a fine coat, which enables you to groom him thoroughly, so that the coat and skin are kept clean. Grooming will also improve his appearance and his circulation.

After picking out the feet, next remove any mud from your pony with a dandy brush. This has quite strong tufts of bristles about 2in (5cm) long, and is the best brush to use on your pony during the winter months. A rubber curry comb, although not essential, can be useful for removing mud as well as the old winter coat. Be careful not to hurt your pony with either of these tools by using them on the sensitive areas of his body; he may react by kicking you.

Then you can get down to the real business of grooming. This is mostly done with the body brush, an oval shaped brush, with soft bristles about 1in (2.5cm) long, with a handle over the back to enable you to hold it correctly. A curry comb is used to clean the body brush and is held in the opposite hand. Start work behind your pony's ears and work backwards, grooming with the direction of the coat. Stand well back from your pony, using a slightly bent arm, so that you can put your full weight behind the brush to reach right through the coat, and down to the skin. Use circular strokes, and every three or four strokes clean the brush by passing it across the curry comb, to dislodge the dirt. The curry comb is cleaned by giving it a sharp tap on the floor or wall. When you have finished one side, change the brush and curry comb into the opposite hands and do the other side, making sure that you have cleaned well under the girth and between the legs. Don't forget your pony's head; be sure you are very gentle, as many ponies are sensitive over their heads. Use just the body brush and make sure that you do not bang the edges of the brush on the bony structure of his face.

The mane and tail need to be carefully groomed; if they are fine, then the body brush is the best tool to use. However, for a pony with a thick matt of a mane and tail, this is not practical, and they can either be done carefully with a dandy brush or a mane comb, making sure you do not break off the hairs in the process. The mane can then be brushed to the correct side with a water brush, although this is not an essential bit of equipment for a pony kept at grass.

You will need two sponges, with a bucket of water. Wash the first sponge and squeeze it out, then carefully sponge out your pony's eyes. Wash the sponge out again and sponge round his muzzle and nostrils. Then, with the second, sponge his dock region, including the skin underneath his tail. Always keep the same

Left A correctly fitted loose-ring snaffle bridle. Beginners should always ride with a snaffle. A bit should be bought to fit the pony's mouth exactly; a snaffle should just wrinkle the corners of his mouth very, very slightly.

Below Equipment needed for a stabled pony, showing a general-purpose saddle with cross-over leather girth; a snaffle bridle with eggbutt bit, drop noseband and ladder reins (to help prevent slipping); a leather headcollar, also available in coloured synthetic material; a blanket and a wool-lined jute night rug, also available in quilted nylon. Grooming kit in a handy carrier – left to right above: stable rubber, two sponges, hoof oil in a tin; below: metal curry comb, rubber curry comb, body brush, dandy brush and water brush.

sponge for each of these tasks – preferably have different coloured ones. You can give your pony a final polish with a stable rubber.

Pulling a mane and tail are rather specialized jobs, and some help from a knowledgeable person is a good idea. Ponies that live at grass need all the protection that they can get for the winter, and manes and tails are best left thick, and not pulled.

Washing your pony

Sometimes in summer it may be necessary to wash your pony, most likely if he is grey and you want to show him. If you do decide to give him a bath, if possible choose a warm day, and give him time to dry before the evening. Make sure you have everything ready that you will need. Use a shampoo made for the purpose; washing detergent is not suitable and can cause skin irritation. Wet your pony with a sponge and a bucket of water, then apply the shampoo and work it well in. The rinsing is most important, as shampoo left in the coat can only do harm. You will need lots of water for this, preferably warm, as your pony is unlikely to appreciate cold water poured over him unless it is in the middle of a heatwave. Begin behind the ears and work backwards, using a brush will help to get the shampoo out of the hair, thoroughly rinse the mane, first of all brushing it to one side, and then brushing it back to the other. Work down both sides of your pony, use a sponge to rinse his face and the sensitive parts of his body.

When you have rinsed all the shampoo out, not forgetting to rinse his tail if you have washed it, then remove as much water as possible from his coat with a sweat scraper. He will probably appreciate it if you dry his head and ears with an old towel, also his heels to prevent them becoming chapped. After this some exercise to help him dry off is a good idea.

YOUR PONY'S TACK

Whether your pony is stabled or lives in the field, you should know how to fit and clean his tack. Do get some expert advice when you buy any tack; regrettably there is a great deal of bad tack available, and this must be avoided. It can be uncomfortable for both you and the pony and also dangerous.

The saddle should fit behind the pony's withers, the lowest point being through the *waist*. Make sure that the cantle is as high or higher than the pommel, otherwise you will always be trying to climb towards your pony's ears. There should be at least $1\frac{1}{2}$in (3.7cm) clearance under the pommel and a 1in (2.5cm) clearance under the gullet, or channel, at the back, so that the saddle does not press down on the pony's spine anywhere.

There are many different kinds of saddles, all designed for a special purpose; but for most riders the *general purpose* saddle is the best to buy at first. It is comfortable to ride on and suitable for many kinds of activity.

For young and inexperienced riders the snaffle bit is the best to use; a jointed eggbutt snaffle is probably the bit most commonly used; it should not pinch the corners of the mouth.

The bridle should fit the pony comfortably, a snaffle bit should be $\frac{1}{2}$in (1.2cm) wider than the pony's mouth and should just wrinkle the corners of his mouth. The throat lash should be done up so that four fingers can be easily slid in. The noseband is fitted two fingers below the bottom of the cheek bones, and so two fingers can be inserted sideways when it is done up. If a drop noseband is used then it must not be fitted low, where it can damage the cartilage structure of the nostrils. A plain cavesson noseband is suitable for most ponies.

All tack is expensive and should be properly looked after to keep it supple, prevent it rubbing your pony and to prolong its life. After it has been used it should be cleaned and put away ready for the next time. Tack that is left with dirt or sweat on it will become hard and will crack.

To clean your tack, you will need some saddle soap; an old flannel is best for applying it. A sponge is needed for washing off the dirt, and a bucket of luke-warm, not hot, water. Take the irons, leathers and girth off the saddle and take the bridle to pieces, wash the bit and the irons in the water. Then squeeze the sponge out in the water and sponge each piece of tack over; be sure to remove all the dirt and grease. This can build up inside the noseband, where the reins and cheek pieces are attached to the bit, and underneath the saddle.

Next you will need to apply the saddle soap. If it is a hard bar of soap, damp it in the water and rub it on to the flannel; if it is a soft type in a tin then just take a little on the flannel. Carefully apply the soap to all the leather work, especially where the leather comes in contact with the pony. When this has been done re-assemble your bridle and saddle and hang them up neatly where you keep them. It should take about half an hour to clean a saddle and bridle, but will probably take longer to begin with. This time will be well spent and will prolong the life of your tack, as well as giving you a sense of satisfaction.

6
ORGANIZATIONS AND RIDING FOR PLEASURE

At a Pony Club Camp in summer, an instructor explains the use of trotting poles.

ORGANIZATIONS AND RIDING FOR PLEASURE

The Pony Club must be one of the largest youth organizations in the world, with over fifty thousand members in Britain, and more than seventy-five thousand members in other countries. The forerunner of the British Horse Society, the Institute of the Horse, formed a Junior Branch known as *The Pony Club* in 1929. The country was broken down into areas corresponding with the hunts, and District Commissioners were appointed for each branch. The membership for the first year, 1930, was seven hundred, so over the first fifty years there has been a remarkable growth to a membership of over a hundred and twenty-five thousand.

The objects of the Pony Club are worthy of mentioning; they are:

1) To encourage young people to ride and to learn to enjoy all kinds of sport connected with horses and riding.

2) To provide instruction in riding and horsemanship and to instil in members the proper care of their animals.

3) To promote the highest ideals of sportsmanship, citizenship and loyalty, thereby cultivating strength of character and self-discipline.

These may sound a little idealistic and not what one immediately connects with the Pony Club, but owning a pony is not like owning anything else. It is by learning the right way to look after a pony and to ride, and the sacrifices that must be made to do so properly, that the character of young people develops.

Few of today's international riders were not members of the Pony Club in their younger days; indeed, the list of former Pony Club members who have represented their country in international competitions must be a lengthy one.

Whilst there is no lower age limit to become a member, most branches do like children to be able to ride a pony to some degree, even if on a leading rein, and five or six years is probably the youngest. Ordinary Members are those who have not attained their seventeenth birthday, after which age they become Associate Members until they reach their twenty-first birthday.

The Pony Club caters for children who have their own pony, or are able to have the use of a pony for rallies. Often a riding school will hire ponies to their regular pupils for these.

From small beginnings, fifty years ago, the Pony Club has indeed grown into a vast organization. A central council meets regularly to decide policies, and there are numerous sub-committees to cover the many different aspects. One of the most successful horse books ever written is the Pony Club Manual, which sells many thousands of copies each year. There is a lengthy list of books and films available for members, varying from educational to humorous and suitable for all age groups.

The backbone of the Pony Club are the working rallies, where children meet together to be instructed in the art of riding and pony management. To encourage members to improve their knowledge and to stimulate interest, a series of standards were introduced and Efficiency Certificates are awarded to members who reach these standards. There are five standards, 'A', 'H' (Horsemasters), 'B', 'C' and 'D', 'A' being the highest and 'D' the lowest. Any holder of the 'A' Test can be rightly proud of this achievement, because a very high standard is required, and there are less than fifty current members who are holders of this certificate.

There are now several national competitions every year, each branch may pick a team to represent them in each competition. These teams will compete against each other at an area level, the winners going on to the national finals.

Pony Club Horse Trials The first of these national competitions began in 1949 and is now known as the Pony Club Horse Trials Championships. The object is to provide a test requiring courage, determination and all-round riding ability. This takes the form of a one-day horse trial, when each competitor must complete three phases, Dressage, Cross-Country and Show Jumping. Penalties for the three phases are added together, to give a result for each competitor, then the best three from the team of four are added together to give a team result.

There is needless to say great rivalry between the members to be selected for this, the most popular of all the national competitions. Although it is called a *horse trial*, (taking its name from the adult equivalent) it has always been designed so that a good pony is equally as capable as a horse of winning.

Prince Philip Cup Mounted Games The next national competition to be introduced in 1957 was the Prince Philip Cup, the Pony Club Mounted Games Championships. This competition has caught the imagination of the public not only in Britain but in several countries abroad. Devised by HRH Prince Philip as a competition for children who had ordinary ponies, probably with no chance of ever gaining a place in the Horse Trials team, it is for members under fifteen years of age. Provided they are prepared to spend the time and take the trouble to train their ponies, almost any animal is suitable.

A series of team competitions was thought out, using variations of the basic gymkhana games seen at many local shows. This competition has become so popular with so many branches entering teams that there now have to be three stages of selection before the finals; the area meetings, the zone finals, then the regional finals when six teams are selected to compete at the Horse of the Year Show at Wembley in October. There excitement reaches fever point as the last night approaches, and all may depend on the result of the last race, as to whether that coveted trophy will be going to the North of Scotland, Wales or stay nearer London. See also page 96.

Pony Club Polo Tournament In 1959 the Pony Club Polo Tournament was first introduced. This is a very specialized sport, and only comparatively few branches enter teams. It has, however, provided a valuable training ground for the sport, for children that otherwise would be unlikely ever to play. The finals are divided into three different age groups for members, under 16, 18 and 20 years.

Pony Club Tetrathlon A competition exclusively for boys was started in 1969, the Pony Club Tetrathlon Championships. It is a challenging competition requiring sound practical horsemanship and general athletic ability.

Run on similar lines to the Olympic Games Modern Pentathlon for men; there are four tests that must be completed by each competitor; they are riding, running, shooting and swimming. The object is to encourage the all-round boy to further his interests in the horse by enabling him to combine riding with other activities.

Pony Club Show Jumping It is perhaps surprising, that, in view of its great public popularity, the Pony Club Show Jumping Championships were not introduced until 1971. Since then they have proved enormously popular, with most of the branches entering teams. The object is to provide an opportunity for branches to compete against each other and to encourage a high standard of riding. It is the team that is important and this competition has done much to create a team spirit in a sport that has unfortunately very often seen both poor standards of horsemanship and very selfish attitudes.

Pony Club Dressage The most recent of the national competitions, the Pony Club Dressage Championship, were finally launched in 1977. Once again these have proved enormously popular, with most of the branches entering teams. This sport, once mainly confined to the rather more elderly, has recently found great support from the young. The object is to show a happy and obedient animal, able to perform a dressage test in a relaxed and accurate manner, also to encourage the riders to ride in the classical school of equitation, and so be able to train their animals to a higher degree.

Pony Club camp It would be very incomplete to talk about the Pony Club without mentioning camps. No less than 305 of the 354 branches in Britain hold an annual camp, with nearly twenty thousand members attending. For many of these children the Pony Club Camp is the highlight of the year. During this time, children not only learn how to ride better than before, but also very important, they learn how to look after their pony, to feed and groom it and to clean their tack correctly. They also learn how to cope with many new situations, to make friends, take orders and also to have fun. Whilst nobody would deny that the weather will make a great difference, pouring rain day after day can be far from fun, there are few children and ponies who do not benefit in some way from even the wettest of camps.

It is perhaps surprising that the Pony Club has not spread throughout Europe as have the Scouts and Guides. In Commonwealth countries there has been a quite remarkable growth. Australia leads the field with over 35,000 members. The competitions there are somewhat different to those in Britain, and include competitions for horses working with cattle, when the marks are awarded on the ability of the horse to cut out a single animal from a herd and take it through a course. New Zealand, Canada and the USA also have a high membership, each country being responsible for the running of its own national organization and national competitions.

For a number of years now, there have been international exchanges between Pony Clubs in different countries, when members from one country spend time as the guests of another country. To gain one of these coveted awards is the aim of many of the more senior members, and can do nothing but good towards a closer international understanding among nations.

The Horse Rangers Association

This exists for children whose parents are less well off, who do not own a pony or have regular riding school lessons. The headquarters are at the Royal Mews, Hampton Court in Surrey and lessons and rides are taken in Bushey Park opposite; there are eight branches around the country. Members are aged six and upwards, and they are taught riding and pony care. They wear an attractive uniform and some help the stewards at horse shows. Naturally it is a popular organization and there is a waiting list to join.

Left Riding in the heart of London, through the arch at Hyde Park Corner into the park, where Rotten Row is long enough for a good canter. It is used by the army from the nearby barracks for exercising their horses, as well as by several riding stables.

Right Hacking in the country on a fine summer day, these two bay ponies are walking in step. The pony on the right has a white star, and is wearing fetlock boots and a standing martingale, which is used to prevent the pony getting his head too high, to a position where he is not under control. When riding on bridlepaths always be ready to stop or slow down for children, elderly people and dogs.

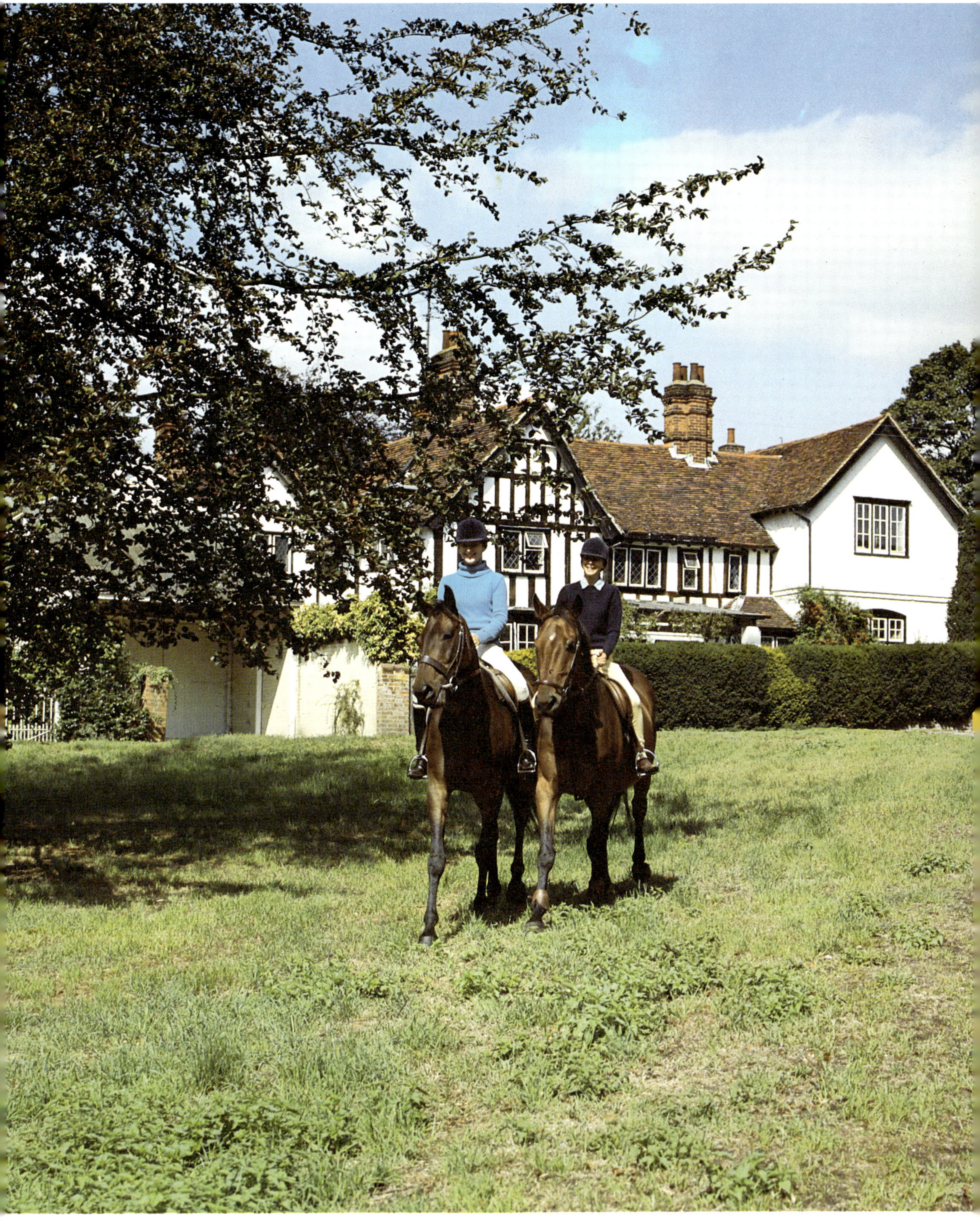

The Endurance Horse and Pony Society

If you have a pony and enjoy the countryside but do not know your area well, it can be more fun to go on an organized 'pleasure' ride, than for a long hack on your own. This society arranges rides of varying distances for all sorts of ponies and riders, over picturesque routes. There are also competitive endurance rides for experienced riders on very fit horses, held under veterinary supervision.

PONY TREKKING

Taking a pony trekking holiday has become very popular over the past twenty years. This form of holiday can now be enjoyed in many countries throughout the world, though it probably originated in Scotland. Naturally the ponies or horses will vary enormously, most of them probably being native to the area in which they are kept. For example a trekking centre on Dartmoor will more than likely use Dartmoor ponies, whilst one in Scotland will use Highland ponies. Similarly in Canada it will be the local stock, and in Norway the native Fjord ponies will fill the bill. Not only are they the best suited and acclimatized to the local terrain, but they are probably the cheapest to buy and maintain.

Trekking holidays are designed for all standards of riders, from complete beginners to those who are quite advanced and able to partake in a lengthy trail ride. What is important is to make sure that you book the right type of holiday that will suit your capabilities. Never be over-ambitious, it will only end in aching muscles, a shattered nerve and maybe broken bones. Also check that the centre is approved by one of the national organizations such as the Ponies of Britain. All too often, young and untrained ponies are equipped with unsafe and ill-fitting tack. Beware of the unscrupulous owners who have no concern for the welfare of the ponies, or sometimes for the riders, and are only in the business to make a 'quick buck'.

Trekking originally came from the Afrikaans word *treck*, meaning a march or migration, and the speed of the journey was that of the ox-wagons. Trekking today has a very different meaning; groups of riders go for daily rides over a planned route, returning to their base each day. Most of these centres are residential and the holiday is all inclusive, with full board and lodging, the use of the ponies, and instruction if it is required.

Most centres will advise those booking holidays of the equipment they will need: a hard hat, proper leg protection such as jodhpurs or chaps to prevent raw or blistered legs, and waterproof clothing.

It is a great help to be able to ride a little before undertaking one of these holidays, and a few lessons at a local approved riding school will be money well spent. For those already able to ride, it will not only refresh them in the art of riding, but will also exercise those muscles that are not normally used in everyday life! There is nothing more miserable than the thought of five more days in the saddle when one is in agony with sore and aching legs and seat.

The attraction of a trekking holiday is that it can be enjoyed by riders of all ages and standards. Most of the route will be undertaken at a walk and only small sections will be negotiated at a trot provided the riders are capable. There are a few centres in Britain that organize *post trekking* for the more advanced riders. The trekkers ride from one site to another each day; they either camp or stay in a hostel or hotel, whilst the ponies are either grazed or stabled overnight. This type of holiday requires much more organization and it is not very easily arranged in Britain.

In America the long-distance trail rides are very popular. Groups of riders, usually riding in Western style, and often on their own horses, ride together for several days along scenic routes. They camp out overnight under the stars, cook their food on camp fires and tether their horses as the cowboys of the West used to do. This requires a high degree of fitness and endurance, and has developed as a non-competitive form of the famous Endurance Rides that were begun in America in 1919.

HUNTING

People have probably hunted in Britain since the Norman Conquest. At first animals were hunted for meat, but over the centuries this has changed. We must define hunting as the pursuit of a wild animal in its own environment by man, with the aid of a pack of hounds. The exception to this is drag hunting, when an artificial trail is laid for hounds to follow.

The fox is the most frequently hunted quarry, although in other parts of the world, jackals, kangaroos, wallabies and deer are also hunted. Britain is considered the home of foxhunting, with more than 200 packs, and numerous packs of beagles, basset hounds and harriers who hunt hares.

Hunting has a very great following among country folk, not only those who are able to be mounted, but also thousands of foot followers, people on bicycles or in cars who follow the hunts. Hunting has received much publicity over recent years, largely because of the actions of people who are against the sport and try to disrupt it. Unfortunately most of these people do not understand the sport and are very ignorant of the facts and the ways of the countryside. Foxes in particular can cause enormous damage, just killing fowls for pleasure and not always because they are short of food. Their numbers must be controlled, but to do this without exterminating them does seem to be done best and most humanely by hunting.

Many young people go hunting every year; it is most essential to get the permission of the master of the hunt before taking your pony. Do make sure that you and your pony are properly turned out. Your pony should be well groomed, the tack clean and correctly fitted, make sure the girth is not too long, because it will need taking up a hole or two during the day. Your pony's shoes must be in good order, and make sure that he is fit enough to cope. If he is not very fit then only stay out for an hour or two.

Cubbing is a good introduction to hunting proper, and starts in August, finishing before the Opening Meet which is in early November. The hunting season ends in April. You can either pay an annual hunt subscription or a 'cap' at the meet.

Young people under eighteen should wear a tweed jacket, either jodhpurs and short boots or long boots with breeches; a collar and tie or hunting tie, gloves and a black velvet hunting cap. Always take a pride in your appearance, your clothes may be second-hand but see that they are neat and tidy, no buttons off or left undone and long hair put neatly in a hairnet.

Be sure to be courteous to other riders and road users; above all respect the property over which you may ride. Always shut gates, avoid riding over crops and repair any damage that you may make to fences. If you are lucky enough to be able to hunt, then it is a very good idea to go with someone who hunts regularly, for the first few occasions at least. They will be able to tell you the *do's* and *don'ts* and show you the best ways to go. After a day be sure to thank the master, and take your pony home slowly, so that he can dry off on the way. He will need extra attention and food after a long day. Remember the rule of water before food, and if possible give him a drink on your way home.

Drag hunting has been introduced in some countries where there is no hunting such as Germany, or in urban areas where it is not possible to hunt. An artificial trail is *laid* usually by someone on horseback, dragging an old sack on a piece of

The winning team at a Prince Philip Cup Mounted Games competition. Each team wears a different coloured vest for easy identification.

Top Ponies taking a drink during a trek in Scotland. Do not allow your pony to drink too much cold water when he is hot, and be watchful that he does not try to roll in the water; some ponies take great pleasure in this.

Above Riders competing in a long distance ride on Exmoor, Somerset. Both pony and rider need to be extremely fit for this type of competition, which is thoroughly organized with strict veterinary supervision. The EHPS and the BHS organize rides to suit many types of pony and rider.

rope soaked with a strong smelling solution. The pack of hounds is then taken to the area where the trail begins, and they pick up the scent. Hounds hunt the trail, with the mounted followers in pursuit, much as a normal hunt. The object is to give riders an opportunity to negotiate natural country; but with an artificial line it is possible to arrange with the local farmers where they may go and so avoid young crops.

Drag hunting is inclined to be a very fast sport, where brave, fit horses are at a premium, it is less suited to children on ponies, who may find the pace and the fences above their capabilities. However, some riding clubs organize 'mock hunts', and some of these will be suitable for less experienced riders.

7
PONY COMPETITIONS AND EVENTS

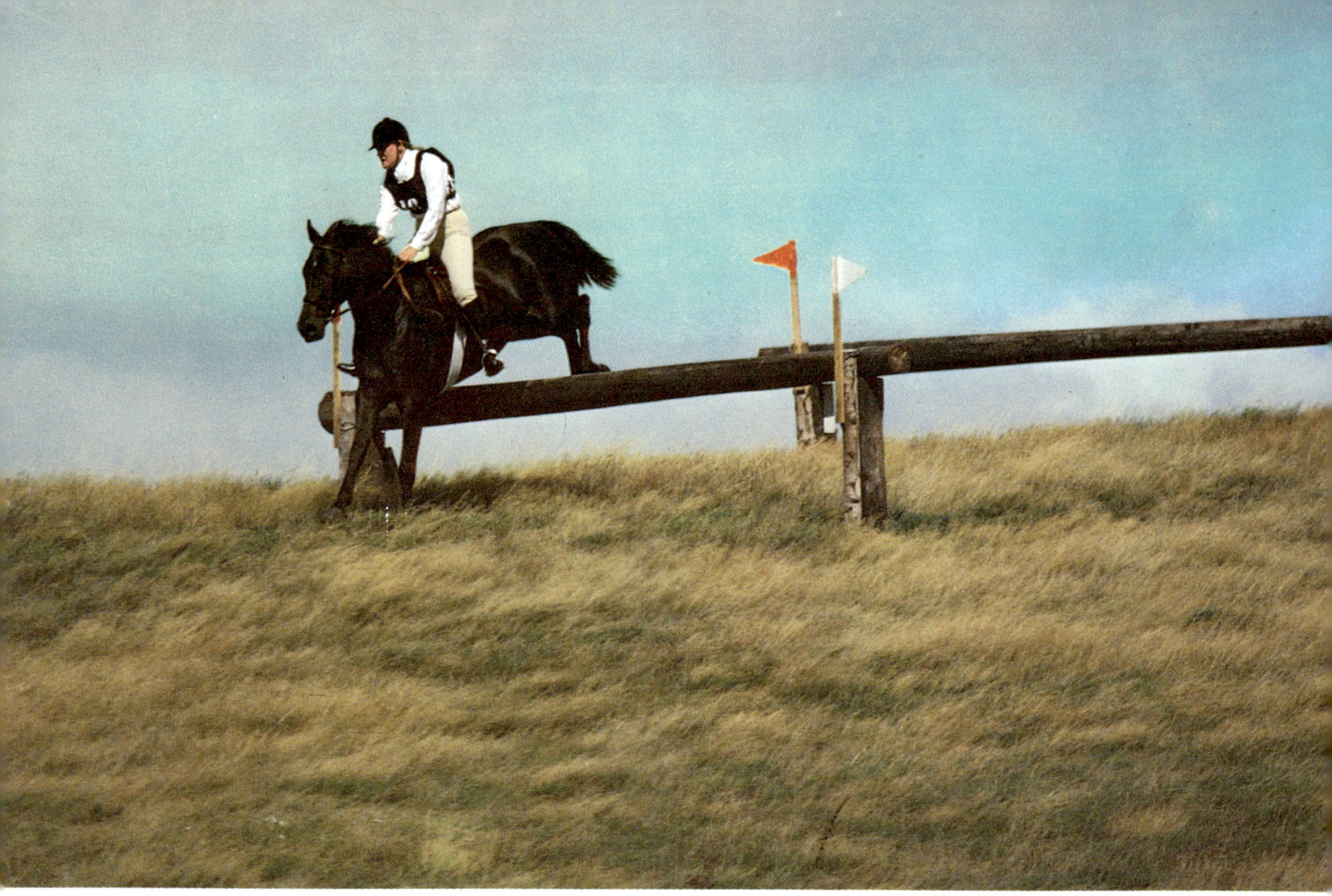

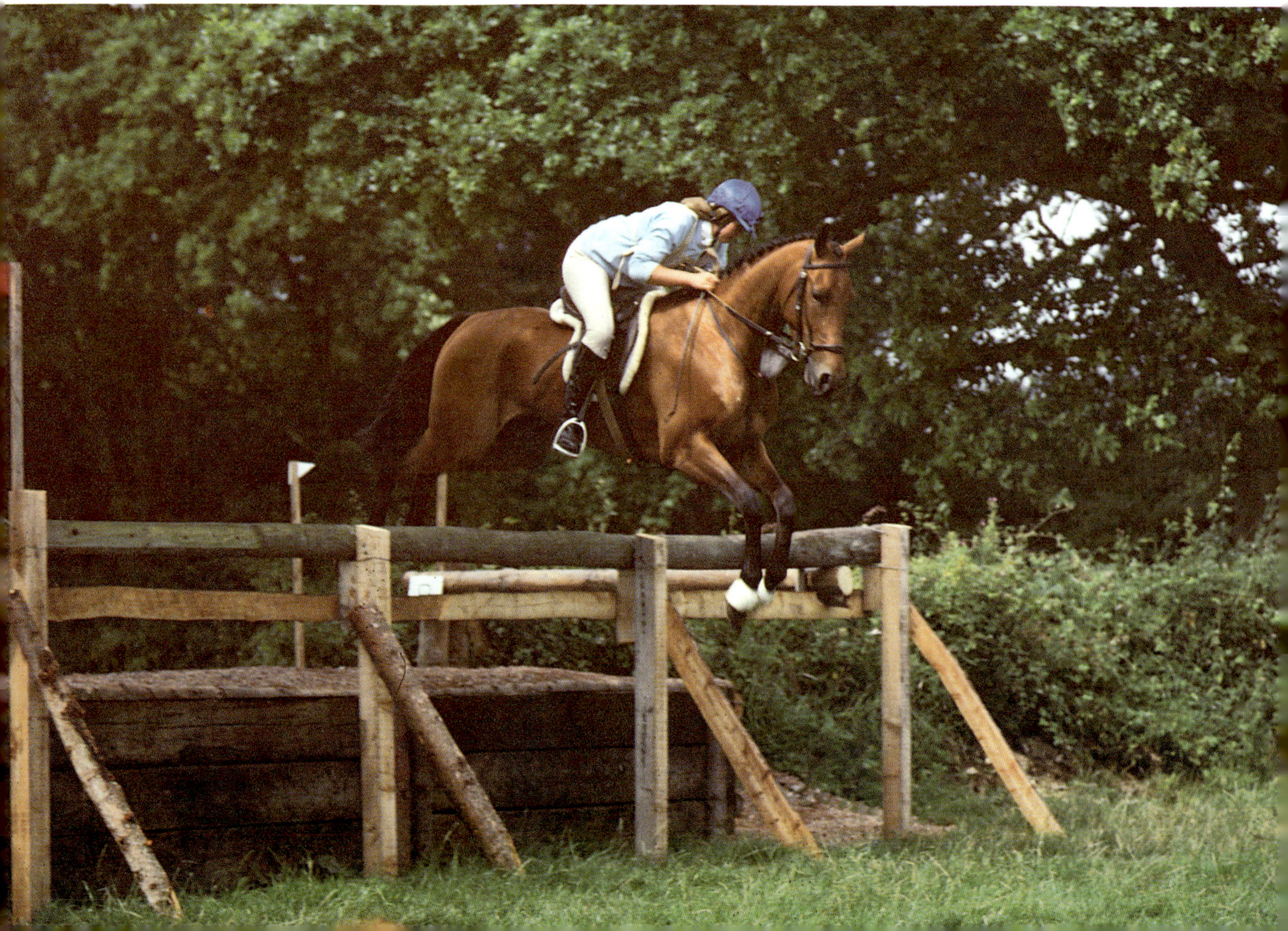

PONY COMPETITIONS AND EVENTS

MOUNTED GAMES AND GYMKHANAS

Mounted games have been part of man's life for thousands of years. Polo is the oldest of the mounted games that has survived; this, together with other mounted games such as tent pegging, were played by the British army in Asia in the mid-nineteenth century, mainly to relieve the monotony and keep horses and riders fit.

In America the Red Indians amused themselves by games played on horseback; a favourite was to tether a live chicken to a stake, then the riders, galloping at full tilt would endeavour to pluck the chicken from the ground. With no saddle and only a leather strip plaited into the mane to hold on to, this required a fair measure of skill.

Many mounted games developed from the work of the local people: for example, most Western sports seen at rodeos in the USA, Latin America and Australia have developed from the work the cowboys used to perform in the nineteenth century.

In Afghanistan a wild tough game called buzkashi is still played; it originated from the nomadic tribes that roamed the steppes. A slaughtered goat or sheep is wedged between a rider's knee and the saddle; he gallops off, then the other players try to wrestle the carcass from him. It can also be played between two teams, who try to gain possession of the beast.

Russia has several forms of mounted sport that are unique: acrobatics on horseback, such as riding backwards or underneath the horse, fighting with javelins on horseback, a form of tennis on horseback, and archery at full gallop as well as tent pegging, are all forms of sport they enjoy.

Pushball, another game played in Russia, is also played in Holland, and the Pony Club have tried it out as well; an enormous inflated ball is pushed along by the teams in an attempt to get it over the goal line.

In Britain mounted games are in the main played by the younger generation. Although some shows have open gymkhana classes, it is for the benefit of the children that these are mainly run. Gymkhanas were introduced to Britain by army officers returning from India, where mounted games had been played for centuries; they became very popular and soon became established at most country shows. The word 'gymkhana' came from India, apparently being a combination of *gymnastics* and *gend-khana*, a Hindustani word meaning ball-house or racket court.

A gymkhana is always fun, but these events can become rough if not properly run, and a good organizing committee who ensure that riders obey the rules is most important.

Provided a pony has been got as fit as possible and is not entered in too many events so that he gets tired, he will nearly always find a gymkhana enjoyable. Ponies who are not particularly good-looking or well-bred have a chance to win a rosette, and it is an opportunity to build up a strong pony and rider partnership.

To be successful at a gymkhana, a rider must teach his pony to be obedient,

Above left This rider is taking the second part of a double, situated on a downhill slope, on a cross-country course.

Left The most demanding part of an event is the cross-country. The rider here is jumping off a Normandy Bank. The pony has overreach boots on to prevent him hurting himself when jumping; they protect the coronet and heel from being bruised or cut by the toe of the hind foot when landing.

supple, quick at turning and nippy. He must obey the aids instantly as every second counts.

Native and crossbred ponies excel in these games. They may not be quite as fast as the near-Thoroughbred ponies, but they tend to be less excitable and easier to cope with when the pressures are on. To have a pony who is steady and accurate is the best policy, and to keep a clear head and quick mind to cope with all the situations that arise will win the day. A willing, unflappable pony, whatever his shape or colour, can help a rider enormously.

Most gymkhanas include the traditional events such as bending, potato race and sack race, and often some specially devised. The obstacle race can be very ingeniously thought-out, but needs a lot of equipment.

In the sack race, a pony who will trot beside a rider, while he endeavours to leap like a kangaroo, can help a lot if the rider can hold on to his neck to balance himself and be assisted over the finishing line. A pony who drags behind and refuses to lead properly can deny a rider a prize. Similarly in the now familiar stepping stones race, a pony who will not keep level with a rider whilst he steps from one tin to the next, can cause him to lose his balance and have to begin again.

There are many strange looking objects used in mounted games, and a pony must become accustomed to all of these. He must also not mind strange noises, the sound of a potato landing in a metal bucket can frighten many ponies until they become accustomed to the noise. The sight of flags flapping or balloons blowing, are all terrifying to ponies used to the quiet countryside, they must be gradually introduced to all these strange sights and sounds.

The old favourite, the bending race, in and out of a line of poles, is run at nearly every gymkhana, in one form or another. It may be used during the delivery and collecting of flags in the flag race.

As well as gymkhana games, mounted games are included at many shows, for the Prince Philip Cup in the Pony Club Mounted Games Championships, described on page 84. This started in 1957, and since that time, the Mounted Games have become overwhelmingly popular, with not only the competitors, but with all the millions of viewers who follow them on television. Strict rules are laid down as to the running of the various games, to the tack the ponies can wear, and the size of rider that may ride small ponies.

The games run in the Prince Philip Cup, as it is known, vary to the usual events at a local gymkhana, they are designed for creating team work, and it is the best team that will win. All the games are constructed to test the skill and the ability of the rider to control his pony, without good schooling and long hours spent teaching a pony, there can be no hope of success.

Working together as a team of riders is very important and requires a lot of practice together to perfect co-ordination. Most races are relays. Ponies and riders alike must be proficient at taking and passing a baton, so many events are won or lost on this. A pony who will not ride face on close to the next pony to give the baton can lose valuable seconds in a race.

The thought of competing at the Horse of the Year Show has inspired thousands of enthusiastic Pony Club members, who patiently school their ponies for these games. To get into a good team is quite an achievement in itself. The team then has to work its way through the Area, Zone and Regional Finals, before the final six teams are selected for Wembley.

Each year different games are selected by a committee, a list of the games with rules being sent to each branch. These must be studied, and the best way of running each race must be found. Cold weekends in January and February seem a long way off to the excitement of the finals in October, but that is when the basic hard work must be done to get the team up to scratch.

EVENTING

Eventing as it is commonly referred to, is a rather vague way of describing one of the fastest-growing and most popular sports on the equestrian scene. Based on an endurance test for military horses that covered three days, it is still known in some countries as the *military*. It was not until the 1920 Olympic Games in Paris that the three-day event took its present form. There was dressage on the first day, on the second day an endurance ride in two phases with the steeplechase in between, followed by a cross-country ride; then on the third day a test of show jumping.

A three-day event obviously requires a very high standard of training and fitness by both horse and rider. A less demanding competition has been devised as a training, this being a modified version taking place on one day. There is a competition each year known as the European Junior Three-Day Event Championships, which is for riders between fourteen and eighteen years old. Each country is entitled to send six riders and horses to these Championships, from which a team of four will be chosen, the remaining two competing as individuals. They partake in a full scale three-day event and it may well be that from among these riders the teams for the Olympic Games will be selected in the future.

Whilst there is enormous competition to get into a team, with several hundred hopefuls partaking in the trials each year in Britain, most of the children probably begin their career on ponies at one-day events, and it is at these we will take a closer look.

Britain holds a unique position in the world with regard to eventing. The adult competitions are almost entirely run by the British Horse Society and are known as Horse Trials, whilst the Pony Club is responsible for running nearly all the one-day events for children and ponies. The first national competition was started in 1949, from when the sport has gone from strength to strength. Huge numbers of visitors watch the very exciting cross-country day at Badminton Horse Trials in April, probably the most prestigious three-day event, and Burleigh, in September, is also keenly followed, both live and on television.

The object of the competition is to test the all-round ability of the pony and rider. There are three stages to the competition, and each rider must complete all three; the penalty marks for each stage are then added together to give an overall result. In many Pony Club events there is a team competition, each branch being represented by a team of four riders, the best three of whom count. This means that if one rider is eliminated, the whole team is not eliminated with him, the score of the other three will be added together for the team result.

Dressage phase

The first section of the event is the dressage when the rider shows the obedience, balance and rhythm of his pony. An arena measuring 40 × 20 metres is marked out on a level field with white boards; around the arena certain points are marked with letters. The riders will come into the arena one at a time and perform a set test; this will have been worked out to show the paces and obedience of the pony at the walk, trot and canter. The judge will sit in a car at one end with someone to write down the marks and comments he or she makes for each movement. These marks are then added up, and are deducted from the maximum marks that could have been awarded to convert them into penalty marks.

Cross-country phase

The second section is the cross-country, to show the endurance and courage of pony and rider. Each competitor is required to negotiate a course of fixed obstacles set in natural surroundings, mostly in hedges or fences. They will be penalized, for

Left This pony is jumping keenly at a local show. To keep up their interest and prevent staleness, ponies should not be asked to jump too often, or too high for their capabilities.

Below The first phase of an event, the dressage, is to show the obedience and paces of the pony. This pony, making a turn to the right, is a little overbent.

Below The flag race at a local gymkhana. The flags have to be collected from a cone and placed in another cone at the end of the course. Speed and agility are essential. The leading pony is wearing a breast girth to prevent his saddle slipping backwards from all the fast movement.

Probably the most famous jumping pony of all, the Irish-bred Stroller, who stands 14.1½hh. With Marion Mould (née Coakes) he won the Individual Silver Medal at the Mexico Olympics in 1968; and previously, the Ladies' World Championship, in 1965. He is now retired and lives on a farm in Hampshire.

any refusals, twenty points for the first refusal at each fence, and forty for the second, the third refusal will mean elimination; a fall of pony or rider is penalized sixty points. There is also a time limit set for the course, worked out on a speed of 400 metres per minute. If they go over this time they will be penalized one point for every five seconds.

Show jumping phase

The third and last stage is the show jumping, when the rider has to show that after the cross-country, his pony is sufficiently obedient and supple to negotiate a course of show jumps. These jumps will not be large compared to the straightforward show jumping classes at shows, but will necessitate several changes of direction to show that the pony is properly under control. Faults for refusals or knock-downs will be added to the scores for the first two phases to give an overall result.

The standards in eventing have been steadily improving over the thirty years that it has been in existence in the Pony Club. There are today many horses competing, basically because their riders are too big to ride ponies, but it has always been the policy of the Pony Club that the course should be constructed so that a good pony should be able to do as well as a horse. Many of the riders will progress to competing in adult competition horse trials; some, as we have said, will take part in the three-day events organized for juniors; others will never reach these standards. However, one thing is almost certain; that those riders who compete in events will be good competent all-round horsemen and women, who will be able to school and train other ponies and horses.

SHOW JUMPING

Show jumping is a comparatively recent sport; the records indicate that jumping contests first began a little over a hundred years ago. However, they bore little similarity to what we are acquainted with today; at a jumping competition in Paris in 1866, it resembled more of a cross-country competition. After a preliminary parade indoors, the competitors were sent into the country to jump, over mostly natural obstacles.

By 1912 at the Olympic Games in Stockholm, international show jumping was well established; although few people at that time would have forecast the remarkable growth that has occurred in the sport since then. Today show jumping is indeed very big business, with not only horses but also ponies changing hands for tens of thousands of pounds. As with eventing, Britain leads the field as far as jumping ponies are concerned, with over 5,500 registered ponies competing at some 1,200 shows.

The British Show Jumping Association (BSJA) is responsible for the running of show jumping in Britain. They draw up the rules and regulations, approve the courses and fences that are used and govern both the judges and the conduct of the competitors.

Most children begin competing in jumping classes at very small shows and gymkhanas. There they have the opportunity to acquaint their ponies with coloured fences, in a ring, with crowds to watch. Once they are able to cope with these small shows, then they probably progress to a class that is run under BSJA rules. It will be necessary then to become a member and to register the pony.

Ponies are graded according to the amount of prize money that they have won. The more experienced ponies, Grade JA, have won more than £150 in competitions.

The less experienced ponies will probably begin by jumping in Junior Foxhunter classes. The height limit for the fences in the first round must not be more than 3'6" (106cm). This means that young ponies can gain experience without being overfaced by fences that are too large for them.

Jumping classes are also divided into different height limits for ponies; these being under 12.2, 13.2 and 14.2 hands high, the children's ages are correspondingly limited to 12 years, 14 years and 16 years.

At a show, the course will be set by the course builder. The first two or three fences should be simple and straightforward to encourage the ponies to jump. There will probably be a combination fence, that is, one fence with two or more parts. Two parts are known as a double, three parts as a treble. If a pony refuses at the second or third part of a combination fence, then he must re-jump the complete fence again.

The competitors will enter the ring one at a time. They must not start before the judge rings the bell. As they go through the start an automatic timing clock will come into operation; as they finish it will stop and record the time they have taken. A certain time is allowed for the course, but if they exceed this time then they will be given time faults.

The scoring for show jumping is rather different to that used for eventing. The fences all knock down if they are hit, and four faults will be given for a knockdown. A refusal will be penalized three faults with six for the second refusal and elimination for the third. A fall of pony or rider scores eight faults.

Those riders who jump the first round clear without time faults will go in for a jump-off, the fences being raised, normally between three and six inches (7–15cm). It is usual that the first jump-off is not judged on time, or, as they say, *against the clock*. However if there is more than one rider to jump this second round clear then the fences will be raised again for a second jump-off. It is most likely that this jump-off will be timed; in the event of equality of faults the fastest time will win.

It is a regrettable fact that show jumping does attract the rougher riders, who are so involved with winning that the welfare of the ponies does not always take top priority. There is also room for much improvement in the standard of riding among juniors, who are frequently seen riding with stirrups that are too long, and hauling unbalanced ponies round the course.

The Pony Club is doing its best to improve the standard of riding, but many children who show jump never bother to become members. It would not be right to leave the impression that all children who show jump are bad riders; those who get to the top are very skilled. The standard of both ponies and riders who reach the finals at the Horse of the Year Show at Wembley in October is remarkably high; the ponies seem to jump incredibly big fences in very fast times.

The pinnacle of the pony show jumping scene must be the European Pony Championships that have been run officially since 1978. A team of four riders compete in these, the best three scores counting for the Team Championship. Competition to be selected is, needless to say, very keen; for those selected it will probably be the first occasion at which they have represented their country in an international competition.

DRESSAGE

The word 'dressage' does, undoubtedly, conjour up in the minds of many people, a sport about which they understand little, and one that is way beyond their capabilities. In fact it is a French word, derived from the verb *dresser*, meaning to train, and dressage does begin at a very simple level, and is within the grasp of anyone prepared to spend a little time training their pony.

Over the centuries dressage has developed in varying degrees in different countries. The Greeks understood the need to train their horses, and a Greek general called Xenophon wrote about the training of their horses in the fourth century BC.

The cavalry of the Middle Ages needed to be able to control their horses with one hand during the battle; for this they needed to be trained. Many of the high school (*haute école*) movements, that may still be seen performed by the Spanish Riding School in Vienna, are the movements that were used in battle hundreds of years ago.

It was during the time of the Renaissance that dressage began to develop more as we know it today. The army used it as part of their training, and many wealthy individuals regarded it essential to be able to ride well as part of their complete education. They used to perform at the Royal Courts and similar centres of culture, but by the beginning of the twentieth century most of the courts had disappeared, which left the army as the main source of knowledge. With the phasing out of most horses from the army by World War II, it was up to the civilians to take up the art. In Britain this has been a very slow process, but over the last few years there has been an enormous increase of interest in dressage, especially among younger people.

Dressage is one of the three equestrian sports of the Olympic Games. Germany has for many years somewhat dominated the dressage scene; with harsh winters, no hunting, and riding confined to indoor schools, it is perhaps natural that they should excel in this field.

It has only been recently that ponies have started to take a more prominent place in the dressage world. Ponies are of course just as capable of performing dressage as horses. The reason that they do not usually reach the same standards is that so much depends on the ability of the rider; few children are able to ride well enough to perform the more difficult movements. The Pony Club has done an enormous amount to improve the standard of dressage among young people. Anyone wanting to compete in horse trials has to do a dressage test for the first phase. It used to be possible to perform a mediocre test, and then get into the prizes by going fast and clear cross-country. That, however, is no longer the case; the standard is now so high and the competition so keen that a good test is essential to

Left These riders are quietly waiting in the collecting ring for their turn at a local show.
Below left For the more experienced child, the first class off the leading rein is the 'Child's First Ridden Pony' class'. This rider is beautifully turned out with leather gloves and a leather-covered show cane. She has safety stirrups.
Below Two Pony Club members, with their badges and ties, correctly turned out for a competition at their local show.

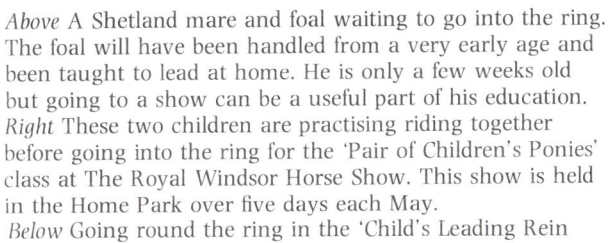

Above A Shetland mare and foal waiting to go into the ring. The foal will have been handled from a very early age and been taught to lead at home. He is only a few weeks old but going to a show can be a useful part of his education.
Right These two children are practising riding together before going into the ring for the 'Pair of Children's Ponies' class at The Royal Windsor Horse Show. This show is held in the Home Park over five days each May.
Below Going round the ring in the 'Child's Leading Rein Pony' class. The leading rein should always be attached to the noseband not to the bit.

stand a chance of a prize. Young people are finding that to have a well-schooled pony is an enormous advantage with the other phases, because a pony that is balanced and obedient is much easier to ride, especially over combination fences.

The European Pony Championships are run over three days, with individual competitions on the first two days, and a team competition on the third day. A full size arena, measuring 60 × 20 metres is used and a high standard is required. Although the more advanced movements that are seen from the horses are not expected, some lateral work and extensions are included in the test. It has been very encouraging to see young British riders in the prize money in the last few years. Let us hope that their example will fire others with the determination and patience that is necessary to reach this standard.

Dressage is a sport in which many people can participate. There are tests and competitions designed for all standards. Anyone who is interested can practise at home with the help of an arena marked out with some old oil drums or markers. Some instruction will be necessary from time to time, because it is not possible to see one's own faults when riding. However, a short period of quiet regular schooling should prove beneficial to most ponies, regardless of whether they are expected to jump or just go out hacking.

SHOWING

The desire of horse breeders to prove that their stock was superior to that of others led to the practice of showing animals of the same species and breed against one another. This began about two hundred years ago, but much the same aims are still present today. If a breeder is able to demonstrate that his stock is considered better than that of other breeders, then not only will he be able to demand top prices, but other owners will want to send their mares to his stallions. Showing classes are either *in-hand* (where the pony is led round) or ridden, but it is always the pony not the rider who is judged. Naturally, though, the rider must be very competent to show the pony to best advantage.

Today showing has spread far and wide throughout the world, and also in the great diversity of the classes. Showing in the purest form must be the in-hand breed classes, but horse shows now put on classes for all types and classifications of animals. Most of them also include classes that are competitive sports, such as gymkhanas and show jumping.

In this book we will consider the showing of ponies, which follows much the same format as that used for horses. Today the pony is probably of greater importance than at any time in history. After all, it had been horses that were used for wars and for transport. In this age of affluence and leisure, more children are taught to ride on ponies then at any time before and this undoubtedly is reflected in the show ring. The ponies in Britain are the envy of the world, and never before has there been the quality or the numbers that we see today. Whilst the native breeds flourish in the show ring, particularly the Welsh Mountain Ponies, it is the Riding Ponies that have increased amazingly since the end of World War II.

As discussed in the chapter on breeds, a Riding Pony is not a breed in itself, but it is a type that has been developed for the show ring. Normally Thoroughbred and some Arab blood is crossed with native ponies, the Welsh and Welsh Mountain being the most popular, to produce an ideal child's pony. Whilst conformation and movement have been of the greatest concern, the temperament has not always been suitable for children. This aspect is now demanding greater attention from the judges of ridden classes.

There are of course the well-known pony studs throughout the world, many specializing in a native breed of pony; there are also many studs now breeding

Riding Ponies. In addition to these studs there are thousands of people who keep one or two mares that are special to them in some way; they select a stallion they think suitable, and then derive great pleasure in following the progress of the youngstock. Many young ponies are taken to a few shows as part of their education and upbringing, to accustom them to the sights and sounds. It is a meeting place for people with similar interests and regarded by many as being as much of a social occasion as one for friendly rivalry.

The native breed classes are usually divided into age groups for the different breeds; yearlings, two and three year olds, brood-mares and foals, stallions and possibly a ridden class, all depending on the number of entries. In the Riding Pony section there are normally classes for three different heights, not to exceed 12.2hh, 13.2hh and 14.2hh at maturity, and each of these heights is then again divided into ages as with the native breeds. Thus a large show may have fifty or more in-hand classes in its programme, requiring much planning and administration.

The procedure for judging in-hand classes is much the same, whatever the breed or size of animal, and follows that used for the in-hand hunters. The ponies are led into the ring and circle around the judge at a walk. They are then normally asked to trot, one at a time, the sideways movement being as important as that seen from behind and in front of the animal.

The judge is looking for the animal that he or she considers is the best of its type, the conformation must be suited to the breed, the movement correct, and the animal must *fill the eye*, as the saying goes. Show animals must also have that hard to define quality known as *presence*, that sparkle that says *look at me, I'm the greatest*.

After the initial walk round the judge will ask the steward to bring the ponies into a straight line in a provisional order. The judge will then look at each pony in turn, inspect it to see that there are no faults such as curbs or splints. The pony will then be walked and trotted in hand so that the judge can see that it moves straight. When all the ponies have been looked at and assessed by the judge, they will once again circle around and then be called into line again in the final order before the awards are presented. The ridden classes are normally divided into height groups of ponies not exceeding 12.2, 13.2 and 14.2 hands high for children up to 12 years, 14 years and 16 years respectively. There may also be a leading-rein class for children under 8 years old on ponies not exceeding 12.0 hands and a first ridden class for children under 10 years, again on ponies under 12.0hh. These ridden classes usually follow a similar pattern.

The ponies will come into the ring one after another and will walk round the edge of the ring. When they are given the signal they will all trot round for a few laps, then again when asked they will canter around. Most judges usually ask them to change direction and canter round the other way as well. They then circle around the judge at a walk and are called into line in a provisional order. Each rider then comes out in turn to give his or her individual show. This is the occasion when the judge can assess how the pony moves, what kind of a ride it appears to give and how obediently it behaves. At this stage the larger ponies will also be expected to gallop.

After the individual shows have been given the ponies will be *stripped* for the judge. At this stage an assistant will be needed to help in the ring. The rider will dismount and take the reins over the pony's head, the saddle will be removed, and the assistant will brush out the saddle-mark and give the pony a final shine. Each rider will in turn take his or her pony before the judge and run it up in-hand the same way as for the in-hand classes. After this inspection the riders will mount again and will circle round the judge before being called into line for the final presentations.

Above This pony, in fine summer condition, is having his hooves oiled and the finishing touches put to his appearance before going into the ring.
Above right A black Shetland stallion shown in-hand. The smallest of the British breeds, the Shetland has proved himself equally valuable in harness as for riding.

Below Young competitors in the fancy dress class. Competitors need not always be mounted for this class, as shown by this gypsy caravan. A pony does not have to be good-looking or a good performer if he is obedient and the handler in control. It is essential to accustom the pony to the strange trappings before the show.

Right A chestnut Riding Pony being shown in-hand in front of the judge, having been 'stripped-off', that is, its saddle removed, for inspection.

Below The winners line up for the judge to present rosettes for the championship at a local show. They will then parade round the ring in a 'lap of honour'. Long hours of hard work and patience go to produce an impeccable turnout like this.

Below right This delightful palomino pony has won the championship and has the rosette on his bridle; the red rosette on his rider's waist is for winning his class, thus qualifying for the championship class.

The leading-rein classes, probably the most hotly contested of all classes at most shows, follow a similar pattern. Each pony will be led into the ring by an assistant on a leading rein that must be attached to the noseband. They naturally will not be expected to canter or gallop. After they have been brought into a provisional line, each will give an individual show. It is then usual for the judge to inspect the ponies while they stand in line, rather than stripping them and running each one up in-hand. Most shows present a rosette to all the riders in the leading rein class. For the very young the thrill of winning their first rosette is a landmark in their riding career.

HUNTER TRIALS

Hunter trials, as the name suggests, are trials for hunters. Riders negotiate a set course, usually laid out on a farm over natural fences. They may be timed over the course, or be judged on style to determine the winner. Most Pony Clubs run hunter trials to give their members the opportunity of riding over a selection of natural fences. The size of these will be suited to the size of the ponies and age of the children, but many courses are now made for riders of ten or under, with larger fences for the older children.

Hunter trials are a very good introduction to riding cross-country fences; these will be met again in the middle phase of events, or if you go hunting. Most ponies enjoy going cross-country, but remember that without the excitement of hounds, the horn, and other members of the hunt, your pony may be less inclined to jump. It is a good idea to school your pony to jump on his own in *cold blood* (without the excitement of a hunt) before you attempt a course. If you can find someone who has some natural fences, arrange for a lesson or two; at first your pony may go better with another pony to give him a lead until he gets his confidence. Remember, the pony must be got into a very fit condition to be entered for hunter trials.

At a hunter trial, walk the course carefully if you are going to ride. Notice the best approach to each fence and note which way you will have to turn after each obstacle. If there is a gate to be opened, then remember that it is the hand nearest the hinges as you approach that is the correct one to use. Practise opening and shutting a gate at home before you go. There will be one or two practice fences for you to use. Let your pony jump them two or three times, but whatever you do, don't tire him out or get him bored by jumping them over and over again. Think of it as saying your tables at school; once or twice is alright, but you would hardly want to spend half an hour repeating the same old thing!

If you are lucky enough to win a prize, then do be sure you are looking neat and tidy to go and receive it. It is hardly good manners to turn up at a prize-giving looking scruffy or sucking a sweet!

8
WORKING AND HARNESS PONIES

Left This cream-coloured pony, driven to a gig, is competing in the obstacle course phase of a driving event. The markers are cones similar to traffic cones, with rubber balls on top; faults are incurred if these are knocked off.

Below This team of Welsh Cobs is on the marathon phase of a three-day driving event, in the Home Park, Windsor. On the first day is the presentation and dressage, the second day the marathon, a course of about 18 miles (29 km), and the third day an obstacle course in the ring. Two grooms must be carried; and passengers may be if the driver wishes.

WORKING AND HARNESS PONIES

As we have said in Chapter 1, horses and ponies were used for work long before they were used for pleasure. At first they were used as pack animals; with a load strapped on their back, they helped the nomadic tribesmen move their goods from one grazing ground to another. Next it was discovered that more could be moved if it was pulled along than if it was carried. At first a pole was attached either side of the pony by means of straps round the neck and girth, and the load was then tied across these poles. The Ancient Britons used these rudimentary sledges; in the forest tracks they probably worked better than wheels. Later chariots with two wheels were used. These would have been used for people to ride in as well as for transport of goods.

The climate and the terrain would have very much affected the use of wheeled vehicles before proper roads were made. In the mountainous parts of the world, pack animals would have been of most use, as indeed they are still used in some areas today. In the more temperate climates, where the winters were wet and where the tracks became muddy, then a cart or chariot would have got stuck in the mud, so once again the pack pony would be best. The dry areas of the Middle East, and southern Europe would probably have been those where the wheel was of most use. Those magnificent roads built by the Romans would also have made the use of vehicles a practical proposition, and indeed the Romans were great traders.

Vehicles were at first used for moving goods, but as time passed, people wanted to use them for passenger travel. The litter was the first method devised for moving people. A box-like construction was attached to poles fore and aft, and these were harnessed to two horses or ponies; this avoided the use of wheels which would have become embedded into the deep ruts in the roads. These were still used during the last century in India.

HORSE-DRAWN VEHICLES

It was not until the middle of the sixteenth century that vehicles were used in Britain for transporting people. Queen Mary Tudor rode to her coronation in 1553 in a four-wheeled chariot pulled by six horses. By the beginning of the seventeenth century the hackney-coach was introduced to London; the word 'hackney' came from the French word *haquenee* meaning a horse for hire. These four-wheeled coaches were much in demand in London and became so popular that they caused great traffic jams!

The eighteenth century can be considered the age of the horse-drawn vehicle. The State Coach in the Royal Mews was built in 1762 and this was followed by many other road coaches. The invention of better springs was the biggest improvement, and meant that passengers could travel in much more comfort. Whilst horses were mostly used for the large vehicles, ponies were by no means forgotten; indeed most households had a pony and trap for all the everyday work.

There were numerous types of vehicles built, many of them being named after their designers, a few of which were built for ponies.

Phaetons

These four-wheeled vehicles were built in different shapes and sizes; small ones suitable for ponies were much favoured by ladies, as they were easy to enter whilst retaining the graceful lines of the larger vehicles. They were open carriages suitable for the owner to drive for pleasure, being driven from a forward-facing seat for the whip (driver) and a passenger. Some were for a single animal, others for a pair and a few for teams of four. Phaetons were used for pleasure driving in towns and parks, Hyde Park being one of the most popular places. Many of these vehicles were built very high off the ground, and were somewhat unsteady. George IV wanted one that was safer and easier to enter, so he had one built for a pair of ponies in 1824. A few years later Princess Victoria had one built for a team of four ponies; these were postillion-driven, that is, the two nearside ponies were ridden by postillions who led the off-side ponies. These two vehicles were soon copied for other ladies to drive and the style became known as a ladies' phaeton.

Gigs

The forerunner of the gig was the sedan cart, a sedan chair on wheels, with the front handles lengthened to form shafts. All gigs have two wheels and most have a forward facing seat for two passengers, the exception being the doctors' gig which had a single seat. There were many different types of gig; most of them were simple unsprung vehicles that were cheap to produce and were used by farmers. As the gig gained in popularity so it was built to higher standards, with springs, and later some had hoods. By the 1830s they were the most common vehicle on the roads, and today they are still one of the most popular vehicles for driving.

The Dog Cart

These vehicles were developed from the gig at the beginning of the nineteenth century, to carry gun dogs on shooting expeditions. Designed to seat four people, the whip and one passenger seated forwards, the other two passengers seated backwards with their feet resting on a tailboard that let down. The dogs travelled under the seats. Most dog carts were pulled by a single horse or pony, but with more passengers a pair was sometimes used, the shafts were removed and a pole fitted for the pair. At first the dog carts were built with two wheels, but later they were found to be more stable and easier to manage with four wheels. They proved such a useful and versatile vehicle that they were used as general-purpose vehicles on most estates. They were the basic shape used by many tradesmen, and farmers for their business. A variety of goods or animals could be put under the seats to go to market, or they could be used for the family for a drive on Sundays.

The Governess Car or Tub Cart

These vehicles were almost always built for ponies and were designed so they were suitable for the governess to take her charges out for a drive in safety. The tub shaped body is entered from the back, the idea being that if the pony moved whilst the children were getting into the vehicle, they would not have their toes run over by the wheels. The door was secured by a handle on the outside, that was out of reach of small children inside; and the sides were built quite high all the way round to prevent anyone falling out. The seats run down either side, facing inwards. The biggest disadvantage is that the pony has to be driven from a sideways facing position, and it may be difficult to control a strong pony.

During the beginning of the twentieth century these governess cars became very popular and were built in large numbers. The quality of them varied enormously, some very fine specimens being built for use in towns and cities by the wealthy; some simple rather rough ones were to be found in the country.

There were of course many other vehicles built, but most of these were designed for horses rather than ponies. The road coaches from which developed the brakes and drags were practically always built for a team of horses. There are a few exceptions, and even today there are still some coaches designed for ponies.

Driving harness

The equipment first used for horses was very simple; ropes twisted out of straw and attached to a sleigh were still being used in Ireland to haul peat in the twentieth century. However, far more sophisticated driving harness had been developed long before then and is still in use today.

It is interesting to note that there was always a harness-room in establishments where horses were kept. Today many people still refer to a 'harness-room', when in fact they mean tack-room. Harness only refers to the equipment used for driving.

Harness varied according to the purpose for which it was required. Ladies driving a smart vehicle in town would want smart and elegant harness to match the vehicle. A pony drawing a milk float would need a practical harness that would stand up to a lot of everyday use. The pit ponies hauling coal in the mines would need a different harness that was suited to pulling the tubs along the mines. All types of harness do have some common factors though; they all have a bridle. This varies quite considerably from a riding bridle; most driving bridles have *blinkers*, stiffened blinds attached to the cheek pieces to prevent the pony seeing to the sides or behind. The more elegant bridles will have brass buckles and brass rosettes for decoration. The bit will be different to those used for riding, and if more than one pony is being driven then it will be essential to have a bar across the bottom of the bit to prevent the sides of the bit becoming caught up in any of the other ponies' harness.

A collar is also essential; this may be a neck collar which is fitted carefully round the neck in front of the shoulders; or it can be a breast collar, a wide band of leather that is fitted round the front of the chest. A saddle, that looks more like a roller, is fitted on the pony just behind the withers and done up with a girth. The rest of the harness is made up mostly of straps, designed to keep the essential parts in place. The vehicle, or load, will be attached to the harness with the traces, the pony pulling most of the weight with the collar.

Ponies that are to be used in vehicles must be *broken to harness*. That is, they must be trained to wear the harness and be taught how to pull a vehicle. At first the harness is fitted and the pony allowed to become accustomed to it. Then the pony will be put in a very rudimentary vehicle and led round so that he gets used to something following him. Gradually he will learn to stop and to start, to turn both ways and to go up and down hills. If he is to be used in a pair or a team he will also have to get used to working with other ponies.

Breeds of harness pony

Whilst nearly all horses and ponies can be both ridden and driven, some breeds are better suited to being driven than others. Probably outstanding among driving ponies is the Hackney, a very elegant pony with an extravagant high-stepping action. Trotting goes far back into history, being mentioned as early as the fourteenth century. Developed in Britain, mainly from Norfolk Roadsters, by the end of the nineteenth century the Hackney was regarded as the finest harness breed in the world. There are both horses and ponies, the ponies proving more popular perhaps today because they are more economical to keep. Hackneys are very distinctive both while moving and standing; the high knee action, with legs thrown well forward after a slight pause of the foot during each stride is

Left The Hackney today is usually only seen in the show ring. The high knee and hock action must be combined with a regular step. This dark bay with three white socks is driven to a show wagon.

characteristic of the breed. When standing they should stand square with the hindlegs well back, covering as much ground as possible. A Hackney pony should be of true pony type, with a neat small head, long well muscled neck, good shoulders and a compact strong body with hard limbs and feet. The most common colours are bay, brown and black.

Other British breeds to prove themselves popular for private driving are all the sections of Welsh ponies, Shetlands and Dartmoors. The heavier breeds, the Highland, Fell and Dale are used more for agricultural work.

Many of the continental breeds are used in harness, the Haflinger and Norwegian Fjord probably being among the most popular. These rather stockier breeds are also in great demand for light agricultural work, the smallholders depending for their livelihood on their ponies.

THE WORKING PONY TODAY

Whilst private driving must be regarded as a sport, many thousands of ponies have been and still are used for work. In Britain the introduction of the internal combustion engine brought about a drastic decline in the number of ponies in every day use; but in some of the poorer parts of the world, ponies may still be found delivering the milk, coal or general groceries. As already mentioned, many people rely on their ponies for doing jobs on their land; collecting hay, hauling logs, ploughing or hoeing between rows of plants, to mention but a few.

Ponies for transport

One place where ponies may still be found between the shafts is in the outskirts of London. The coster ponies, who pull the carts for their owners, the costermongers,

Above right Disabled riders being given tuition by a Horse Rangers instructor.

Right Being led around the stable yard. Helpers are all volunteers and include senior Rangers. Two or more are usually needed for each disabled rider for mounting and dismounting.

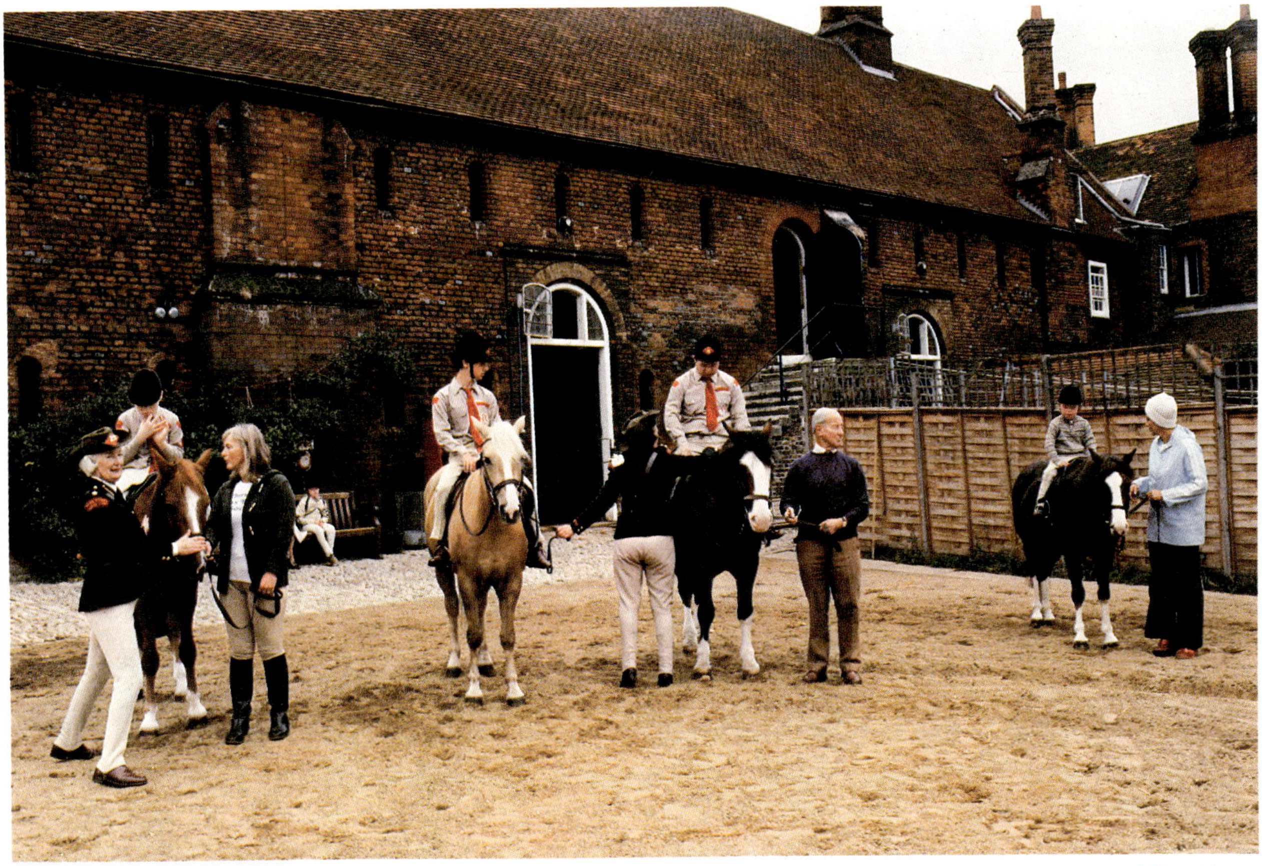

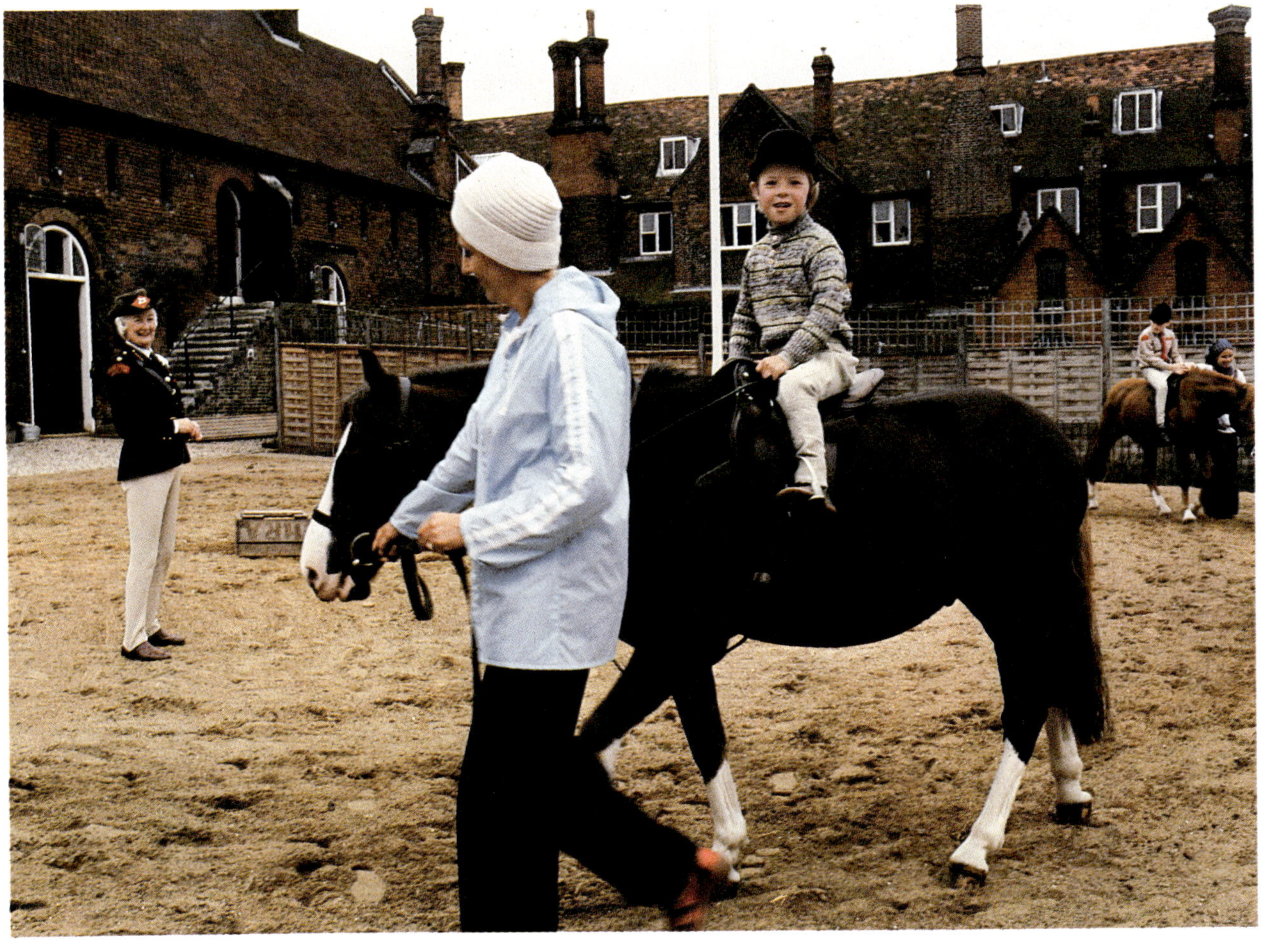

have a special class to themselves at the Royal International Horse Show held at Wembley in July each year. They are the last relics of a thriving trade when coster ponies could be seen pulling carts piled high with fruit and vegetables through the city streets.

Over the past century, thousands of ponies were used to transport various goods. Many of them were used as pack ponies, the Fell ponies amongst them, carried lead from the inland mines to the ports on the north east coast of Britain. Ponies were also used to carry live fish in brine, from the sea ports to inland cities such as Coventry as well as the much more usual cargoes that had to be moved from one place to another. In South Africa pack ponies are still in use to take goods up the mountain tracks where trucks are unable to go.

In Scotland, Highland ponies are used to cart the stags down from the mountains. Once again, they can go where there are no roads, and where all forms of mechanized transport are of no use.

For several hundreds of years the army has relied on horses and ponies for the movement of all its supplies, either on wagons or on pack animals. Today it is only those places that are least accessible where the pack pony is still used by armies.

Without ponies to work in mines, the history of the world may have been very different. Undoubtedly they played a very important part in the industrial revolution, because without coal in large quantities, the incredible change from hand-made goods to machine-made goods could never have happened. It was not until the nineteenth century, when cages were constructed to lower into the mines, and horizontal workings were made, that pit ponies were used. Then thousands of small ponies, many of them Shetlands or Shetland crosses, were used in the mines to haul truck loads of coal from the working face to the shafts where it was raised to the surface. In some cases this was a matter of miles rather than yards. Today this is all done by machinery and the pit pony no longer has a place in the mining industry; the last British pit ponies were retired in 1972 from a Yorkshire mine.

Ponies for herding

So far we have discussed working ponies that are used for driving or transporting goods, but there are of course thousands of ponies that are used for work in other ways. Many shepherds rely on their pony to see their flocks of sheep on the mountains each day. In Britain one may see ponies used by shepherds on Exmoor and Dartmoor, as well as in Wales, the Lake District, Northumberland and many parts of Scotland. In Europe it is true to say that where there are sheep in mountainous regions, there will be ponies used to look after them.

In other parts of the world, such as Argentina, ponies are used for herding the cattle. The gauchos (cowboys) regard their ponies as sacred and their most valued possession. None of the traditional Wild West scenes of wild horses for them; the foals are handled from a very early age, the gauchos have learned to gentle a horse forever with kindness instead of brutality. A young horse will then be tied to an older horse to learn the work before he is ever ridden. A horse that bucks is regarded as a disgrace for its trainer; it is a pity that more people who train horses do not heed the ways of the gauchos.

Ponies in entertainment

Ponies have for many years been used for entertainment. The main attraction of a circus used to be the horses and ponies. Shakespeare refers to a horse that 'danced' before the crowds, so we can assume that performing ponies have been used for several hundred years. It was not until the nineteenth century that the circus as we know it today came into existence. The days when the great names of Bertram

Mills and Billy Smart, who both staged lavish productions, alas, have gone. They both kept stables full of exquisite horses and ponies to enthral the crowds; however, the advent of television bringing the glitter into people's own homes brought the downfall of such expensive shows. The circuses of today are smaller and usually travel round the country, thus avoiding the expense of large permanent sites. In other countries circuses continue to draw big crowds, such as the Moscow State Circus which features daring riding acts by Cossacks and Turkmens.

Ponies are always a favourite for films. Horses have been used for Westerns since film making first began, but the interest now is probably more in the less dramatic scenes than of guns and Indians of the frontier days. Television has again had a great influence with many films being made for television serials, often using children with ponies in the cast.

The pantomime is yet another field of entertainment where ponies are in demand, Cinderella without her coach pulled by a team of ponies would just not be right!

RIDING FOR THE DISABLED

A different field where ponies have proved of great benefit is that of disabled people. The Ancient Greeks used to put crippled people on horses after the Games; and they have presumably been moved throughout the ages by horses, as the only form of transport. It was not until after an outbreak of poliomyelitis in Britain in 1957 that the idea was born, much inspired by the example of Danish rider Liz Hartel, a polio victim who rode in the 1952 and 1956 Olympics. It was thought that the endless and boring exercises that these children had to do would be much more exciting if done on a pony. This proved so successful that the Advisory Council of Riding for the Disabled was formed in 1964. In 1969 the work was taken over by the Riding for the Disabled Association, a registered charity depending on voluntary helpers. There are now more than 500 registered groups throughout Britain. Some of these are attached to riding schools, some to residential homes for the disabled, but many rely on individuals with their own ponies to help once or twice a week for groups of disabled people. Whilst it is mainly children who are helped to ride, there are also a number of disabled adults, many of whom now prefer to drive a pony and trap rather than ride.

Nearly every type of disability can be catered for; some modifications to the saddlery may be necessary, longer reins for armless children, or basket saddles for those without legs. Probably the most usual form of disability is spasticity in children; it is not then a case of adapting tack, but of providing another stimulation.

The dramatic improvements that have been witnessed in disabled children has astounded many doctors. The emotional and psychological benefits are enormous. Children who have never spoken a word in their lives, after a few riding lessons have amazed people by suddenly beginning to talk. The physical improvements vary from a general improvement in well-being to an unbelievable improvement of muscular use and control.

The ponies used must be carefully selected and *bomb-proof*. They will have to be unperturbed by unusual sounds and movements of their riders. At first it is usual to have three assistants, one to lead the pony and one each side to help the rider. As progress is made, depending on the degree of disability, some riders will be able to manage their ponies on their own. This will obviously give their morale a great boost, and help them through the struggle of life until the next lesson. Riders do develop a great feeling of understanding between themselves and the ponies.

Certainly many of the ponies seem to understand that although the riders are not always in control, they must co-operate to the full.

Since the organization began in Britain, it has been adopted in 43 countries throughout the world, helping children of different ages, colours and creeds.

It is possible only to mention a few of the ways in which ponies have served mankind throughout the past four thousand years. Without doubt man would never have made the progress that he has without the help of horses and ponies. They have carried him into battle, helped him conquer lands and build empires. Industry and many forms of business have depended on ponies. They have been both servant and friend to countless generations of people, and although their role in the future may change, if the time should come when there are no ponies, it will indeed be a sad one for mankind.

This fine chestnut Welsh Cob (Section D) has white socks on his forelegs and white stockings on his hindlegs; he is showing a nice extended trot, harnessed to a 'trade turnout' in a driving class.

Glossary

Andalusian: Spanish breed of quality horse descended from Moorish Barbs and local stock, developed by 15th century Carthusian monks.

Appaloosa markings: a variety of spotted markings; may be dark spots on a white background, or white spots on a dark background.

bay: any shade of brown with black 'points', that is, mane, tail and legs, below knees and hocks, see page 31 and 114.

bone: measurement of cannon bone just under knee.

cantle: back of saddle.

cast: describes a pony which is stuck on its back with four legs in the air, unable to get up.

cavesson: for lungeing, a padded headcollar with noseband, throatlash and attachment for lunge line; also, an ordinary noseband on a bridle.

chestnut: variety of shades from light golden to fairly dark or liver chestnut; see pages 22, 34 and 118.

clean limbs: legs without a lot of feather and free of major blemishes.

Clydesdale: heavy draught horse of Scotland, slightly smaller than the Shire.

cobby: stockily built equine with a rounded barrel, short cannons and good bone.

cold-blooded: describes heavier, working type of horse and pony breeds.

collected walk, trot and canter: describes a manner of going in which the pony flexes his neck and brings his hock well under.

colt: a young male horse or pony.

condition: physical fitness and appearance.

daisy-cutting: action at walk or trot which is close to the ground, with little elevation.

dished: describes horse or pony's face which is slightly concave, like the Arab's.

dorsal line (also known as eel-stripe): dark line down centre of back.

dun: variety of sandy colours: grey duns, yellow duns, golden duns and mouse duns; must have black mane and tail and legs below knees and hocks; see page 6, 30 and 31.

eel-stripe: see dorsal line.

feather: long hair on lower legs.

flaxen (mane or tail): a pale or cream colour, usually on chestnut horse or pony; see pages 2 and 6.

floating: trotting action which looks as though horse is on air and springs, characteristic of Arab.

girth, depth of girth: depth between back bone and breast bone.

green: describes horse or pony who is inexperienced and only partially trained.

hand: 4 inches (10 cm); hh means 'hands high'; roughly the width of the palm plus thumb, by which a horse's height was traditionally measured.

hot-blooded: describes the Arab and Thoroughbred.

length of rein: denotes the length of rein between the bit and the hands; an animal with a good front, that is, a fairly long neck and good shoulder, which will take a good length of rein.

lungeing: circling horse or pony on long rein; used for training, also teaching riding.

Oriental: Arab and Barb horses.

overbent: describes pony with its nose tucked into its chest, behind the vertical line from the poll to the nostrils

palomino: gold colour with silvery white mane and tail; see page 107.

Percheron: heavy draught horse originally from France, with very little feather.

piebald: black and white in irregular patches; see page 47.

pony: equine under 14.2 hh.

quarters: hindquarters.

roan: mixed white hairs with another colour; blue roan, white hairs with black; strawberry roan, white hairs with brown; and red roan, white hairs with chestnut.

Shire: heavy draught horse, one of the biggest horses in the world, descended from medieval 'Great Horse'.

skewbald: any colour except black, with white in patches.

stud: breeding establishment.

stud book: the official breeding records kept by the governing body of each breed.

sickle hocks: those that appear curved like a sickle from side view, a fault of conformation.

sulky: very light two-wheeled harness vehicle with seat on an arched axle, on which driver sits, his feet on the shafts.

trotting (races): racing in harness, nowadays using sulkies.

waist (of saddle): narrowest part of the saddle about 3 in (8 cm) behind pommel.

warm-blooded: describes horses bred from both hot and cold-blooded ancestors.

Address List

Pony Club: British Horse Society
British Equestrian Centre
Stoneleigh
Kenilworth
Warwickshire   CV8 2LR
Where to ride list of approved riding
   schools; mail-order bookshop.

Association of British Riding Schools
Mrs M. Simlo
Chesham House
56 Green End Road
Sawtry
Huntingdon
Cambridgeshire   PE17 5UY
List of approved riding schools.

Pones of Britain
Mrs E. Geffers
Ascot Racecourse
Berkshire
*List of Approved Trekking and Riding
   Holiday Centres.*

English Riding Holidays and Trekking Association
Homestead Farm
Charlton Musgrave
Wincanton
Somerset
List of approved establishments.

Horse Rangers Association
Miss D.L. Kirby
The Royal Mews
Hampton Court Palace
East Molesey
Surrey

Endurance Horse and Pony Society
Mrs J. Connolly
Garden Flat
Mynthurst Leigh
Reigate
Surrey

Riding for the Disabled Association
Miss C. Haynes
Avenue R
National Agricultural Centre
Kenilworth
Warwickshire   CV8 2LZ

Byeways and Bridleways Trust
9 Queen Anne's Gate
Westminster   SW1

Horse and Pony (fortnightly magazine)
subscription dept
Competition House
Farndon Road
Market Harborough
Leicester

Pony (monthly magazine)
D.J. Murphy (Publishers) Ltd
104 Ash Road
Sutton
Surrey   SM3 9LD

Riding (monthly magazine)
subscription dept
Oakfield House
Perrymount Road
Haywards Heath
West Sussex   RH16 3DH

The Horseman's Bookshop
J.A. Allen and Co
1 Lower Grosvenor Place
Buckingham Palace Road   SW1W 0EL
Catalogue and mail-order.

UNITED STATES OF AMERICA

United States Pony Clubs
303 High Street
West Chester
Pennsylvania 19380

American Horse Council
1700 K Street, NW
Washington   DC 20006

Points of the horse

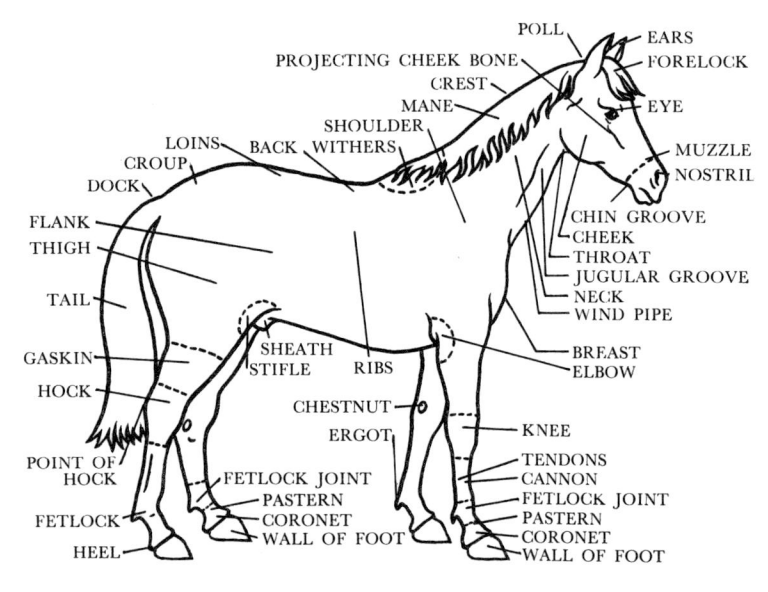

Index

Page numbers in *italic* refer to illustrations

aids 45, 49, 51, 52
ailments 67–8, 76
American Shetland 36
Arab *10–11*, 13–14, *15*, 36, 39, 104
Australian Pony 40
Avelignese 29

bandages *67*, *71*
Basuto 36
Bhutia 38
bots 73
bridles *42*, *78*, 79–80

Camargue 18, *19*, 20
canter 56, 60
Caspian *34*, 39
Chincoteague 36–7
clipping 68–9, 72
clothes, riding *42*, 43, 89
conformation 12, 104
Connemara 27, *31*
cracked heels 72
Criollo 38
cross-country 57, 60, 84, *94*, 97, 99, 101, 108

Dales 21, *23*, 114
Dartmoor 25, *26*, 28, 88, 114
disabled, riding for 18, *115*, 117–18
dressage 84, 97, *98*, 101, 104
driving 111–14, *118*
   breeds 18, 29, 114
   competitions *110*
   harness 113
   trotting races 33, 36
   vehicles *110*, 111–14, *118*
Dülmen 20

eventing 84, *94*, 97, 99, 100
exercises *47*, 48–9
Exmoor 16, *19*, 25

Falabella 38
feeding 63, 65, 67–9, 71, 76
feet 12, 68, 71, 76
Fell 21–2, *23*, 114, 116
fields 63–5
   fencing 63
   grazing 63, 65, 68
   poisonous plants 64
   shelter 63

water 64, 67, 68
Fjord 29, *30*, 88, 114

Galiceno 37
Garrano 32
Gotland 33
grazing 63, 65
grooming *23*, 68, 77, 79, 89, *106*
   kit 77, *78*
Gudbrandsdal –Døle
   Gudbrandsdal 29
gymkhanas 95–6, *98*, 100

Hackney 36, 111, 113–14
Haflinger *2*, *6*, 18
hay 63, 65, 67, 71
Highland 20–1, *23*, 88, 114, 116
Horse Rangers 62, *70*, 85, *115*
horse trials, see eventing
Hucul 32
hunter trials 60, 108
hunting 9, 68, 89, 101
   drag hunting 89, 92

Icelandic 28
Indonesian ponies 38–9

jumping 54, 57, 60, *94*, *98*, 99, 108

Kathiawari 38
Kazakh 39–40
Konik 32

lameness 72, 76
laminitis 68

Marwari 38
Mongolian Wild Horse, see Przewalski Horse
mounted games 95–6
   Prince Philip Cup 84, 90, 96
mud fever 72

New Forest 25, *31*

Pony Club 82, 83–5, 90, 95, 97, 99, 101, *102*
Pony of the Americas 37
Przewalski Horse 6, 9, 14, 16, 32, 39

riding lessons *42*, *46*, 47, 55
Riding Pony 28, 104, 105, *107*
riding schools 43, 83, *86*, 88
rugs 69, *71*, 72, *78*
   stable *71*, 72, *78*
   New Zealand 69, *71*

Sable Island 37
saddles 79–80
Shetland *3*, 20, *22*, 36, *106*, 114, 116
shoes 76, 89
showing classes *102*, *103*, 104, 105, *107*
   in-hand *103*, 104, 105
   leading rein *103*, 108
   ridden 104, 105
show jumping 84, 85, *98*, 99, 100, 104
shows *23*, 65, 66, 96, 100, 101, *102*, *103*, 104, 105, *106*, *107*, *110*, *114*, *115*
snaffle bit *42*, *78*, 79–80
Sorraia 32–3
Spiti 38
stables 66, 69, *70*, 71, 74–5
sweet itch 68

tack *78*, 79–80, 88, 89
Tarpan 9, 16, 32, 33
teeth 73
tetanus 73
Thoroughbred 13, 14, 28, 65, 104
trekking 88, *91*
trot 53, 55–6
trotting poles 56, *82*

Viatka 40

walk 52, 53
water supply 64, 67, 68, 71
Welsh Mountain Pony 22, 27, 104, 114
   Pony 24, 28, 104, 114
   Pony of Cob Type 24, 114
   Cob 24, *110*, 114, *118*
worms 73

Yakut 9, 40

121